QUEST OF FAITH

Understanding What You Confess

Robert De Moor

CRCPUBLICATIONS

Grand Rapids, Michigan

Acknowledgments

The Education Department is grateful to Robert De Moor for writing this course. Rev. De Moor is pastor of First CRC in Langley, British Columbia.

Library of Congress Cataloging-in-Publication Data

De Moor, Robert. 1950–
    Quest of faith: understanding what you confess / Robert De Moor.
        p.   cm.
    1. Reformed Church—Doctrines—Miscellanea.   2. Reformed Church—
Catechisms. I. Title.
BX9422.2.D45   1989
238'.57—dc20   89-15769
                                                              CIP

5 4 3 2 1

ISBN 0-930265-74-2

Contents

Introduction

This brief review of Reformed teachings is intended primarily for anyone of high school age or above who wants to "think through" and deepen his or her faith.

AUDIENCE

Quest of Faith is especially aimed at those about to profess their faith. Many will read and discuss this book as part of a pre-confession, or "pastor's," class. Others will use it to guide their personal study and reflection as they prepare for their interview with the church council.

The quests that appear on these pages are questions council members might ask during a profession of faith interview. The suggested answers are not the only "right" answers, but they should promote thinking and talking about the questions and searching for one's own answers—within the Reformed faith.

Quest of Faith is also an excellent resource for council members who are about to participate in a profession of faith interview. It will help them ask the kinds of questions that elicit knowledgeable and sincere responses.

However, *Quest of Faith* needn't be used exclusively in "profession of faith" settings. Churches might choose to present this book to inquirers about the Reformed faith; they'll appreciate its clear format and simple explanations. Persons from non-Reformed traditions who have recently joined the church will find *Quest of Faith* a useful guide to the beliefs of their new congregation and denomination. And adult church school classes will profit from taking a deeper look at their faith as they discuss many of the questions raised in this book.

FORMAT

The sixty-five quests in this book were selected not only to prepare persons to profess their faith but also to deepen their insights and faith-responses to Reformed Christianity. Each quest offers several possible answers for personal reflection or for discussion. The answers conclude with "The Church Says," an example of how the church's creeds, confessions, and other formal statements of faith have responded to each question. Most of the selections are taken from the Heidelberg Catechism, the Canons of Dort, and the Belgic Confession; several come from *Our World Belongs to God*, a contemporary confession of faith of the Christian Reformed Church, and *Our Song of Hope*, a contemporary confession of faith from the Reformed Church in America.

"The Church Says" is followed by "Hotseat Questions," which are designed to stimulate readers beyond standard answers and pat phrases to deeper, personal responses. An additional section, "Check It Out," provides a sample of Bible references for further study. Participants may want to use these references for personal devotions during the week.

GROUP SESSIONS

Quest of Faith has a flexible format that can be adapted to meet the needs of a variety of classes and groups. Its sixty-five quests are divided into seven major topics, each with ten quests (except for the final chapter, which has five quests). Most classes using the material will probably meet seven times (ten quests per session); groups preferring a slower pace can take five quests per week, for thirteen sessions; groups desiring an in-depth study could take only one or two quests per week, for up to a full year of weekly sessions.

Leaders should adapt the material to the interests and abilities of students. Pre-confession students should not be left with the impression that they must have an instant answer to all sixty-five quests; the intent is for the students to think through their faith, not memorize it. Assignments of quests to be read at home should be reasonable for all participants.

Leaders should select questions for discussion that are most important and interesting for their students. Questions that students have on the material they've read should get top priority. "Hotseat Questions," too, should provoke considerable reflection and discussion.

Leaders will find it useful to frequently ask students—especially pre-confession students—to answer questions in their own words. For variety, leaders may occasionally want to assign a student to prepare thoroughly on just a single quest from the chapter, then present that quest to the group for discussion. Statements from the creeds and confessions can be used to summarize a given quest.

In some cases, especially when working with younger students, leaders may want to provide one-on-one tutoring, perhaps not requiring students to read the textbook but rather using it as a leader's resource to help them frame questions for discussion.

We think *Quest of Faith* is flexible enough to satisfy a variety of audiences and purposes. We hope that studying and discussing these questions and answers will help all readers to speak more clearly and honestly of the hope they have in Christ.

The Education Department

From the Beginning

(Quests 1–10)

<table>
<tr><td>QUEST
1</td><td>How do you know God is real in your life?</td><td>*If God is not real, making profession of faith is just a big joke. And if God does exist but ignores us, we would be foolish to commit our lives to him; we might as well pack in all the fun we can before death robs us of everything. Only if we're sure that God lives for us will it make sense for us to live for him.*</td></tr>
</table>

Some Possible Answers

I feel his nearness in worship, prayer, or song. God often makes us feel close to him through experiences that "grab" us. For example, a song may strike a deep chord in our hearts, making our spirits soar with his. But because our feelings can lead us astray, this very real way of experiencing God cannot be the only way.

I see him in the wonders of the universe and the beauty of a rose. We understand so much about artists from their art. Similarly God shows us much about himself through creation. Swirling galaxies show his power, the elegant rose his skill. But this important way of experiencing God cannot be the only way we know him. Unless we know God more personally, we will overlook his telltale signature on the things he has made.

Looking back, I see how he guides my life. Despite the setbacks, our lives may show God's guiding hand. Through everything he gives us—home, friends, experiences, even bad times—we see he works in us and for us. We glimpse how God fits together the pieces of our lives. Of course, we cannot depend fully on this way of knowing God either. Life may throw us a curveball. Things may happen to us that we will never understand this side of heaven. Especially in those times we need a surer way of knowing we have a God who cares.

My parents taught me about God. God uses parents as a major way of telling us about himself. But this answer begs another question: Where do parents get this knowledge?

God reveals himself through the Bible. The Bible is the clearest and most reliable way in which God speaks to us. Through many witnesses it tells us the great things only he could have done. By telling us God sacrificed his Son and raised him from the dead, the Bible assures us of two things: First, God lives. Only he could raise Jesus from the dead. Second, God cares. He gave us his only Son so that we may live with him forever. That fact makes our lives eternally important.

The Church Says

We know God by two means:
First, by the creation, preservation, and government of the universe,
since that universe is before our eyes
like a beautiful book
 in which all creatures,
 great and small,
 are as letters
 to make us ponder
 the invisible things of God:
  his eternal power
  and his divinity,
  as the apostle Paul says in Romans 1:20.
All these things are enough to convict men
and to leave them without excuse.
Second, he makes himself known to us more openly
by his holy and divine Word,
as much as we need in this life,
 for his glory
 and for the salvation of his own.

(Belgic Confession Article 2)

Hotseat Question

When do you pay attention to God, when he *SHOUTS* or when he whispers?

Check It Out

Psalm 19:1–7; Romans 1:18–23; 2 Peter 1:12–21

<table>
<tr><td>

QUEST

2

</td><td>

What do you really need to know about God?

</td><td>

Our understanding of God determines our response to him. If we see him as an angry, demanding tyrant, we will not love him. If we view him as the jolly, Santa-Claus type, we will not take him seriously. And if we see him as a weakling who helplessly watches his world self-destruct, we will not trust him. To get along with God we need a clear picture of who he really is.

</td></tr>
</table>

Some Possible Answers

God is almighty. God is Spirit. He needs no eyes to see, no ears to hear, no hands to act. Unlimited by time or space, he has no beginning and no end. He can do whatever he wants and be wherever he pleases. Nothing and no one can stand in his way. He always accomplishes what he sets out to do and leaves no loose ends. He is so powerful that our lives and our futures are fully in his hand.

God is the Great I Am. His covenant name, I Am Who I Am, assures us that God always remains faithful to the promises he makes to us because he always stays the same. He will not and cannot lie, cheat, change his mind, or break his promises. We can fully rely on everything he tells us. Because receiving his promises is worth every sacrifice, we venture out in faith, doing what he tells us to do. He is the one sure thing in our lives.

God is triune. As three sides make up one triangle, so Father, Son, and Holy Spirit make up the one true God. Though we cannot fully grasp it, that mystery makes us see God for who he really is and what he does for us.

God is holy. God lives in unapproachable light. As sinful, imperfect creatures we can never reach God on our own. Nor will his justice allow God to sweep our sins and disobedience under the rug. We cannot coast along in life without seriously dealing with our relationship to him. By ignoring his holiness we commit spiritual suicide. But like a powerful bleach, his complete purity holds out to us the promise that he can make us clean like himself. If we believe, he will wash us in the blood of his Son.

God is love. The deepest mystery we discover about God is his all-embracing love by which he binds us to himself. As a baby's life depends completely on the loving care of his parents, so we depend with our whole being on God's love. In John 3:16 we discover how deeply God cares for us: "For God so loved the world that he gave his one and only Son, that whoever believes in him shall not perish but have eternal life."

The Church Says

> I believe in God, the Father almighty,
>   creator of heaven and earth.

> I believe in Jesus Christ, his only Son, our Lord,
>   who was conceived by the Holy Spirit
>   and born of the virgin Mary.
>   He suffered under Pontius Pilate,
>   was crucified, died, and was buried;
>   he descended to hell.
>   The third day he rose again from the dead.
>   He ascended to heaven
>   and is seated at the right hand of God the Father almighty.
>   From there he will come to judge the living and the dead.

> I believe in the Holy Spirit,
>   the holy catholic church,
>   the communion of saints,
>   the forgiveness of sins,
>   the resurrection of the body,
>   and the life everlasting. Amen.

(Apostles' Creed)

Hotseat Question

Where have you let your picture of God get lopsided?

Check It Out

Exodus 3:13–17; John 1:1–8; John 3:13–21

<table>
<tr><td>QUEST

3</td><td></td></tr>
</table>

Why is it important to you that God created everything?

We need to look at our roots. Where we come from tells us who we are and where we are headed. This turns out to be truest of all when we look at the big picture: where did the universe itself come from? Because we belong to this world, the question turns into an intensely personal one: Why are we here? Does our life on this planet make any sense? Or are we just useless blobs of tissue infecting a tiny dust ball lost in the empty blackness of a meaningless existence?

Some Possible Answers

Because it gives my life meaning. Many people believe the universe never had a beginning, that it always just was. They maintain that mere chance throws eternal stuff into ever-changing patterns that have no purpose. Everything happens by mere accident and will always continue to drift in endless variations that never get anywhere. Such people maintain that we are nothing more than temporary creations of that unthinking, uncaring mess. We have no reason for being. We just are.

Against this hopeless, bleak view the Bible reassures us that things do not just happen: a good, loving, all-powerful God has created all things. He continues to control and to care for all he has made, including us. God carefully designed us and formed us. He destines us to live forever with him in perfect fellowship. That gives us a future to really look forward to.

Because it assures me he'll see me through everything the world can throw at me. The apostle Paul writes:

> I am convinced that neither death nor life, neither angels nor demons, neither the present nor the future, nor any powers, neither height nor depth, nor anything else in all creation, will be able to separate us from the love of God that is in Christ Jesus our Lord.

Romans 8:38–39

Because it challenges me to care for this world. Because he made it, God asks us to treat his world with care and respect. Like a true artist, God created the universe to express his genius, vision, and skill. Then he designed us to enjoy it, praise him for it, and make it even better. He invites us, as his coworkers, to develop and unfold its riches. He calls us to care for his seals, whales, wolves, and condors. He allows us to take what we need to live but not to loot, rob, foul up, or destroy his good earth.

The world remains his, and so do we. He has every right to ask his daughters and sons to help in the family business: making the world a place that gives him the glory he so richly deserves.

The Church Says

The eternal Father of our Lord Jesus Christ,
    who out of nothing created heaven and earth
        and everything in them,
    who still upholds and rules them
        by his eternal counsel and providence,
is my God and Father
        because of Christ his Son.

I trust him so much that I do not doubt
    he will provide
        whatever I need
        for body and soul,
    and he will turn to my good
        whatever adversity he sends me
        in this sad world.

He is able to do this because he is almighty God;
he desires to do this because he is a faithful Father.

(Heidelberg Catechism A. 26)

Hotseat Question

Does your life-style destroy or build up God's world?

Check It Out

Genesis 1:2–3; Psalm 148; Acts 17:22–31

| QUEST 4 | Why did God put you on this planet? |

Too many rock videos scream at us that we're here just to have fun. Nobody, including God, objects to good, clean fun. But when our whole lives revolve around fun, we miss the boat. Making pleasure all-important turns into a dreary, disappointing bore. We miss the excitement of knowing that what we do really counts. Sooner or later we bump into the truth: we're not here just to have a good time. God made us for a higher purpose, and we'll never be really happy until we find it.

Some Possible Answers

He made me to glorify him. God created us to look beyond our own needs and wants. He asks us to look up at him. He showers us with gifts and surprises. He wants us to discover them and say thanks with a new song, a fresh approach, a job well done. He calls us to take the effort to enrich the lives of others, too, so that they also will praise him. Jesus challenges us: "Let your light shine before men, that they may see your good deeds and praise your Father in heaven" (Matt. 5:16).

He made me to serve others. God put us on this planet for others. We're not supposed to be little islands separated from each other by oceans of selfishness. He made us interdependent, not independent. When I serve you and you serve others, we become more than scattered bricks. God begins to build us into his temple.

He made me to do work. God made us in his image. We reflect him not by what we look like but by what we do. Through our work we rule the world for him. Although dolphins may have bigger brains than we do and killer whales a richer vocabulary, God has put us in charge of the world. He invites us to work with him to develop the world into a place even more beautiful and glorifying to him.

He made me to be happy. God made us his children, not his slaves. What we do, we do for him, for others, but also for ourselves. God designed us to be daughters and sons who enjoy helping out in the family business. He calls us to manage his good earth. Unless we take that challenge, we'll never be happy. Like a child allowed to help Dad drive the tractor, the work *itself* enriches us; not just the payment we receive for it.

He made me to help build his kingdom. God did not bench us because we blew our assignment. We don't have to sit around waiting for God to clean up the mess we made of our lives. He invites us to help rebuild ourselves and the world we ruined.

Jesus tells us: "I chose you to go and bear fruit—fruit that will last. Then the Father will give you whatever you ask in my name. This is my command: Love each other" (John 15:16–17).

The Church Says

God created them [people] good and in his own image,
    that is, in true righteousness and holiness,
so that they might
    truly know God their creator,
    love him with all their heart,
    and live with him in eternal happiness
for his praise and glory.

(Heidelberg Catechism A. 6)

Hotseat Question

What does God call you to do with your life?

Check It Out

Genesis 1:27–30; Micah 6:6–8; Matthew 28:18–20

<table>
<tr><td>

QUEST

5

</td><td>

Why does God let bad things happen to you and your loved ones?

</td></tr>
</table>

When life hums merrily along, we find it easy to believe in a loving, all-powerful God who controls all things. But when tragedy shatters our well-being, we cry, "Why, God, why do you hurt us so?" Some claim God is punishing us for our sins. But the Bible clearly tells us that Jesus paid the penalty for our sin in full. Others claim God is powerless to prevent Satan from hurting us. But the Bible denies this too. God always has the upper hand over evil. Believing the opposite would make our suffering even worse. A dentist's drill may hurt us more than a mugger's blade, but we find the former easier to bear because we know it hurts us for a good reason. In the same way, the Bible assures us, "we know that in all things God works for the good of those who love him" (Rom. 8:28).

Some Possible Answers

God corrects me. Parents discipline their children to keep them on the right track. So does God: "My son, do not despise the LORD's discipline and do not resent his rebuke, because the LORD disciplines those he loves, as a father the son he delights in" (Prov. 3:11–12).

God wants to teach me something. "No pain, no gain" can apply outside the gym as well. Our best learning may take place with our backs up against the wall. We may find the experience highly unpleasant, and God certainly takes no delight in hurting us, but sometimes when he places us in a sink-or-swim situation, he makes us grow like crazy.

God strengthens my faith. Like flabby muscle, faith that has never been tested can remain immature and weak. The painful questions that well up inside us when we hurt can toughen our commitment. Often when life treats us like fancy crystal, our faith breaks easily. But when God allows life to kick us around like a football, our faith bounces right back.

God prevents greater harm. A child may think the nurse who pokes him with the big needle is very mean. But a pinprick now may prevent a lifetime of misery. God too sometimes sends hardship, even death, to snatch the final victory over us out of Satan's jaws.

God may benefit others. God sometimes sends us suffering as an opportunity to serve others. The way we endure our pain can help us reach the unreachable. Many times believers have preached the good news more effectively from a hospital bed than a pulpit.

I don't care as long as God knows. As children who cannot understand why the surgeon's scalpel has to dig so painfully deep, we may never understand why our Healer brings such grief. But we do not need to know why. We trust the One holding the knife. *He* knows what he's doing. That's good enough for us.

The Church Says

> Providence is
> > the almighty and ever present power of God
> > by which he upholds, as with his hand,
> > > heaven
> > > and earth
> > > and all creatures,
> > and so rules them that
> > > leaf and blade,
> > > rain and drought,
> > > fruitful and lean years,
> > > food and drink,
> > > health and sickness,
> > > prosperity and poverty—
> > all things, in fact, come to us
> > > not by chance
> > > but from his fatherly hand.

(Heidelberg Catechism A. 27)

Hotseat Question

Is God responsible for the suffering you cause yourself?

Check It Out

Psalm 73; Romans 8:28–39; Hebrews 12:4–13

<table>
<tr><td>

QUEST

6

</td><td>

Why does God allow you to disobey him?

</td><td>

Decisions, decisions—life constantly confronts us with new choices. So does God. Why? Why does he give us the chance to make bad decisions? Why does a good God give us enough rope to hang ourselves? Surely he could have made us incapable of evil. Why didn't he?

</td></tr>
</table>

Some Possible Answers

God wants me to be free. God made us different from the animals by creating us in his image. He didn't want the crown of his creation to be driven by animal instincts and brute desires. So he gave us a will that can overcome our natural inclinations. By giving us the ability to make choices, God places us in a unique relationship to him. In all our decisions he looks for our yes to him and our no to all else.

God wants children, not robots. Unless the batteries conk out, a robot will unquestioningly follow instructions. But sooner or later its limited responses disappoint us. It can only do what it has been programmed to do—no more, no less. God expects more from us. He made us to be his children. Like any parent, God knows that his children will bring him a lot of pain because they will not always obey. Yet he considers the risk worth it. God denies himself the emotional safety of creating toys. His father's heart yearns for much more than that.

God wants me to show that I love him. Forced love remains unconvincing. If God forced us or manipulated us to do what's right, we could never prove our love to him. He has to give us the chance to opt out. That's a risky business! But the times we freely choose for him are worth the pain of our failures. By giving us his own Son, God fully showed us how much he loves us. Now he daily awaits our loving response—not because we have to, but because we want to.

God treats me as a covenant partner. God seeks open agreement. He does not put a gun to our heads and force us to serve him. As he keeps his promises to us, so he expects us to keep the promises we make to him. He takes us at our word. He will not stoop to pulling rank in seeking our obedient response. He'll warn us. He'll try to persuade us. But he won't force us. That would violate the way a covenant God relates to his people.

The Church Says

We believe
that God created man from the dust of the earth
and made and formed him in his image and likeness—
   good, just, and holy;
   able by his own will to conform
   in all things
   to the will of God.

But when he was in honor
he did not understand it
and did not recognize his excellence.
But he subjected himself willingly to sin
and consequently to death and the curse,
   lending his ear to the word of the devil.

(Belgic Confession Article 14)

Hotseat Question

Which decision in your life most clearly shows your response to God?

Check It Out

Genesis 3; Joshua 24:19–27; Hebrews 12:22–29

QUEST
7

List some excuses you've given for sinning. Why don't they wash?

By nature we bark up the wrong tree. Instead of facing up to our sin and dealing with it, we try to gloss it over with pious excuses. We pretend that by hiding our sin, we can undo it.

But God looks straight into our hearts. If we continue to deny our sin, his righteous judgment will crush us. Only by dropping the baloney and openly admitting our guilt can we overcome sin's fatal consequences.

Some Possible Answers

It wasn't so bad. Like criminals who think nothing of bumping off another victim, we blind ourselves to the real consequences of our sin. Because sin is a way of life for us, we easily ignore its devastating effect on an eternal, holy, perfect God. He loves us so much that even our smallest misdeeds inflict more grief on him than we can ever imagine.

The devil made me do it. God gives Satan the power to tempt us. But he cannot overpower us. He can talk us into disobeying God only when we let him. James assures us: "Submit yourselves, then, to God. Resist the devil, and he will flee from you" (James 4:7).

I had good reasons for doing it. On God's green earth no reason can ever be strong enough to justify hurting him. He commands us to love him above all else. Any patch-up job that disobeys God's clear commands only inflicts more injury on God, on our neighbors, and on ourselves. It only bogs us down more deeply in the mess we've made.

Our sins are always stupid, senseless, and *un*reasonable.

I meant well. The road to hell is paved with good intentions. God has every right to expect right actions along with good intent.

It didn't hurt anybody. The Bible denies the possibility of a victimless crime. Sin tears God apart and brings his curse down on our heads.

God made me this way, so I couldn't help it. True, we did not choose to be born as sinners in a broken world. But we cannot blame God for our sin either. He created humankind perfect in every way. He rightly holds us accountable for what Adam and Eve got us into. They were our representatives. We inherited from them our weakness for sin, which we willingly plunge into every day.

I didn't know it was wrong. Any police officer knows the answer to this one: "Ignorance of the law is no excuse . . . in fact, it makes you doubly guilty. You should have known." Paul writes, "The wrath of God is being revealed from heaven against all the godlessness and wickedness of men who suppress the truth by their wickedness, since what may be known about God is plain to them, because God has made it plain to them" (Rom. 1:18–19).

The Church Says

**Will God permit
such disobedience and rebellion
to go unpunished?**

Certainly not.
He is terribly angry
   about the sin we are born with
   as well as the sins we personally commit.

As a just judge
he punishes them now and in eternity.

He has declared:
   "Cursed be every one who does not continue to do
everything written in the Book of the Law."

(Heidelberg Catechism Q. & A. 10)

Hotseat Question

What makes it so hard to confess your sins?

Check It Out

Genesis 3:8–19; Psalm 32; 1 John 1:8–10

<table>
<tr><td>

QUEST

8

</td><td>

What false hopes do people have of avoiding God's judgment on sin? How do you respond to them?

</td><td>

Nobody enjoys the prospect of confronting an angry God. We hate to face the music for our guilty deeds. So we hide behind rosy notions about him that let us avoid dealing with reality. That makes us feel good but delivers a lethal sting. Like cancer patients who refuse to admit their illness, our denial makes us refuse the only medicine that can really cure us. The cop-outs we invent prevent us from turning to Christ.

</td></tr>
</table>

Some Possible Answers

I live a pretty decent life. Close isn't good enough. A holy, perfect God, who invests so much into us, has the right to expect perfection. Besides, the idea that we can pretty well measure up to God's demands is sadly misguided. He expects us to love him with all our heart, soul, mind, and strength, and our neighbor as ourself. None of us even comes close to fulfilling those requirements.

    The Heidelberg Catechism puts it this way: "Can you live up to all this perfectly? No. I have a natural tendency to hate God and my neighbor" (Q. & A. 5).

The good I do makes up for the bad. It doesn't. What we do may be good in the eyes of others but not in God's eyes. By his measure even our best works fall far short of what they should be. Offering our works to him to pay for our sins is like trying to pay a traffic ticket with Monopoly money. The catechism puts it up front: "Are we so corrupt that we are totally unable to do any good and inclined toward all evil? Yes, unless we are born again, by the Spirit of God" (Q. & A. 8). The works acceptable to God don't show up in our lives until after our sins are already paid for!

It's God's own fault for making me the way I am. The catechism also cuts off this dead-end attempt: "Did God create people so wicked and perverse? No. God created them good and in his own image . . . so that they might truly know God their creator, [and] love him with all their heart" (Q. & A. 6).

God asks too much. He'll lighten up. Again the catechism denies this escape: "Doesn't God do us an injustice by requiring in his law what we are unable to do? No, God created humans with the ability to keep the law. They . . . robbed themselves and all their descendants of these gifts" (Q. & A. 9).

God is merciful. He'll let it go. When all else fails, we throw ourselves on the mercy of the court: God is merciful. Maybe he will sweep our sins under the rug or let us off with a tap on the wrist.

God's mercy does not work in that unjust way. He levies the full punishment our sins deserve. His mercy beams through instead in the gift of his Son. Jesus pays the penalty for those who stop copping out and take the real road to forgiveness that he provides.

The Church Says

> According to God's righteous judgment
> we deserve punishment
> both in this world and forever after:
> how then can we escape this punishment
> and return to God's favor?
>
> God requires that his justice be satisfied.
> Therefore the claims of his justice
> must be paid in full,
> either by ourselves or by another.

(Heidelberg Catechism Q. & A. 12)

Hotseat Question

Are you totally corrupt right now?

Check It Out

Psalm 51; Isaiah 53:5–8; John 3:1–8

| QUEST 9 | If God is so loving, why can't he just ignore your sins? | *Most North Americans have the silly notion that God is just a jolly old Santa Claus in the sky. They think he will turn a blind eye toward their sins because of the good things they do. God is love, they say. But because they do not understand God's love, they hang on to a false security that prevents them from seeing how much they need Jesus. We may not make that deadly mistake.* |

Some Possible Answers

God always keeps his word. God does not lie. When he makes a promise, he keeps it. When he makes a curse, he keeps it too. God does not make idle threats. Therefore, he cannot simply ignore our sins. From the beginning he has made it crystal clear that he will punish sin: "You must not eat from the tree of the knowledge of good and evil, for when you eat of it you will surely die" (Gen. 2:17). We have to take God's warnings seriously. He does.

God is just. Judges who "fix" parking tickets may appear to be merciful, but they're actually unjust. It is unfair to exact the full penalty from some violators and let others off the hook. For the same reason, God cannot just ignore our sins. His perfect righteousness demands that our penalty be paid in full.

God is a jealous God. The more deeply we love someone, the stronger the hurt, anger, and bitterness we feel when they betray us. Our sins hurt God as deeply as a wife's adultery tears apart a loving husband. Precisely because he loves us so deeply, our sins make God angry. The flip-side of God's love is his righteous, fierce jealousy for our hearts and lives.

God's love seeks a pure relationship. People who really care about each other will not just continue to stumble along in a partnership that has been dirtied and wounded by unfaithfulness. They either openly confront their spiritual separation or they doom their relationship. Their only hope for a fresh start rests in a good scrubbing of their relationship. That hurts. But true lovers will settle for nothing less.

In the same way God refuses to tolerate what we have made of our bond with him. He loves us too much to limp into eternity with us in a so-so partnership that causes more friction and pain than it's worth.

The Church Says

But isn't God also merciful?

God is certainly merciful,
but he is also just.
His justice demands
   that sin, committed against his supreme majesty,
   be punished with the supreme penalty—
   eternal punishment of body and soul.

                                         (Heidelberg Catechism Q.& A. 11)

Hotseat Question

Would you be impressed if God treated you the way you treat him?

Check It Out

Deuteronomy 28:15–20; Psalm 5:4–6; Ephesians 5:3–7

| QUEST 10 | Do you see yourself as a sinner or a saint? |

Knowing yourself presents you with a difficult challenge. You need to walk the razor-sharp line between an inferiority complex and conceit. The struggle is important because the way you look at yourself strongly affects the way you feel, think, and act. It affects the way you treat others as well as yourself.
The need for an appropriate self-image extends also to your spiritual life. Do you see yourself as a sinner or a saint? Your answer shows a great deal about your relationship to God, your neighbor, and yourself.

Some Possible Answers

I'm a sinner. We need to know we are sinners so that we will embrace Jesus as our Savior. Knowing how deeply we sank makes us truly thankful to him for what he has done for us. This gratitude motivates us to commit our lives to him.

However, even after we've committed our lives to Jesus, we still fall into sin. He has not yet fully released us from the old nature that still clings to us. Knowing our sinfulness prevents us from becoming spiritual snobs. Daily we recognize our dependence on God's grace. John writes: "If we claim to be without sin, we deceive ourselves and the truth is not in us. If we confess our sins, he is faithful and just and will forgive us our sins and purify us from all unrighteousness" (1 John 1:8–9).

I'm a saint. We may not sell short the saving work of God in our lives. By grace, through faith, we have been cleansed by the blood of Jesus, and we are new creatures. We confess that of ourselves we were totally corrupt and unable to do any good at all. But God, through the work of his Word and Spirit, has already given us a new nature. We are born again, able now to live for God. Paul wasn't kidding when he addressed his letters to the *saints* in every church.

Both. Luther rightly called believers sinners *and* saints—at the same time. That doesn't seem very reasonable. How can we be totally corrupt and totally perfect at the same time? Yet the Bible tells us that deep down, believers are already the pure, loving, sinless new creatures they one day will fully become. In this life our dirty old selves still hang onto us. Like an emerging butterfly, we still drag around the old skin of what we once were. Therefore we need to keep killing off the sinner in us and bringing out the saint.

Paul warns us: "We have an obligation—but it is not to the sinful nature, to live according to it. For if you live according to the sinful nature, you will die; but if by the Spirit you put to death the misdeeds of the body, you will live, because those who are led by the Spirit of God are sons of God" (Rom. 8:12–14).

The Church Says

> **But are we so corrupt**
> **that we are totally unable to do any good**
> **and inclined toward all evil?**
>
> Yes, unless we are born again,
> by the Spirit of God.
>
> (Heidelberg Catechism Q.& A. 8)
>
> **What is involved**
> **in genuine repentance or conversion?**
>
> Two things:
> the dying-away of the old self,
> and the coming-to-life of the new.
>
> (Heidelberg Catechism Q. & A. 88)

Hotseat Question

Where in your life do you really experience the struggle between the "new you" and the "old you"?

Check It Out

Romans 8:1–17; 2 Corinthians 5:14–21; Colossians 3:1–17

God's Choice

(Quests 11–20)

QUEST
11

Who do *you* say Jesus is?

Nothing stinks more of spiritual death than the empty compliments Jesus gets from those who refuse to believe in him. They cook up pious, high-sounding phrases such as "great teacher," "first creature," "real revolutionary." But these wafflers make Jesus vomit: "I know your deeds, that you are neither cold nor hot. I wish you were either one or the other! So, because you are lukewarm . . . I am about to spit you out of my mouth" (Rev. 3:15–16). Jesus refuses to let us cop out. Either we fully accept his claims or we take him for a liar, a nut, or a blasphemer spouting God-insulting baloney. With tough love he warns us to get off the fence. He daily seeks our answer in word and deed: "Who do you say I am?"

Some Possible Answers

Jesus is my God. Only if Jesus is truly God dare we entrust him with our life in this world and the next. Therefore the Bible clearly spells it out:

> In the beginning was the Word, and the Word was with God, and the Word was God.
>
> John 1:1

> "The virgin will be with child and will give birth to a son, and they will call him Immanuel"—which means, "God with us."
>
> Matthew 1:23

> Who, being in very nature God, did not consider equality with God something to be grasped. . . .
>
> Philippians 2:6

> Do not be afraid. I am the First and the Last. I am the Living One; I was dead, and behold I am alive for ever and ever.
>
> Revelation 1:17–18

Jesus is my brother. Jesus is no ivory-tower wise guy. He became one of us. He understands our weaknesses, struggles, sufferings, and fears because he shared them. As our friend, he takes our side. Jesus invites us: "Come to me, all you who are weary and burdened, and I will give you rest. Take my yoke upon you and learn from me, for I am gentle and humble in heart, and you will find rest for your souls" (Matt. 11:28–29).

Jesus is my Savior. We embrace Jesus as our loving Savior who rescues us from the misery our sins have brought us. Through his gift of himself Jesus grants us salvation full and free. He proclaims, "God did not send his Son into the world to condemn the world, but to save the world through him" (John 3:17).

Jesus is my Lord. We obey Jesus as the Lord of our life. Through his glorious and gentle reign we shall live forever in loving harmony with God, each other, and all creation. Paul writes: "God . . . gave him the name that is above every name, that at the name of Jesus every knee should bow . . . and every tongue confess that Jesus Christ is Lord, to the glory of God the Father" (Phil. 2:9–11).

The Church Says

> We believe . . . in one Lord Jesus Christ,
>> the only Son of God,
>> begotten from the Father before all ages;
>>> God from God,
>>> Light from Light,
>>> true God from true God,
>> begotten, not made;
>> of the same essence as the Father.
>> Through him all things were made.
>> For us and for our salvation
>>> he came down from heaven;
>>> and was made human. . . .

(from the *Nicene Creed*)

Hotseat Question

How, where, and when in your life did you embrace Jesus?

Check It Out

Daniel 7:13–14; Matthew 1:18–25; John 20:30–31

| QUEST **12** | Why do you call Jesus your Savior? | *We call Jesus "Savior" because he saves us from our sins. That good news sums up God's yes to all our hopes, dreams, and longings. We cannot begin to imagine all the effects his saving work has on our lives. We list only a few.* |

Some Possible Answers

Jesus saves me from the punishment I deserve. Like mass murderers, we can never fully pay for our sins. The injury we cause the eternal, holy, just God would rightly keep us in hell forever. But "the punishment that brought us peace was upon him" (Isa. 53:5). On Golgotha he took our place. He removed the guilt of our sins by paying the penalty in full.

Jesus fulfills the obedience I owe God. Jesus fulfills all righteousness for us. He gave God all the things that he expects from his well-created children. Though our sin made us bankrupt before God, Jesus clears our God-account by his total devotion to the Father. For us he remained faithful to the bitter end.

Jesus saves me from slavery to Satan. By goading us into sin, Satan wormed his way into a position of iron-fisted rule over us. He uses this power to make us ruin God's good earth. And, like drug addicts who cannot help choosing over and over again the poison that kills, we let him. Jesus has to wrench us back—will, heart, and soul—from Satan's death-grip so that we can serve God again.

Jesus saves me from chance. Like a bulldozer gone berserk, this sin-wrecked world brings senseless chaos into our lives. But Jesus restores meaning to our existence. He makes whatever happens to us fulfill God's purpose. He takes our failures, sufferings, triumphs, and joys and turns them to our ultimate good.

Jesus saves me from the power of death. Jesus conquered death for us. Death, once the iron gate that locked us forever in hell, is now the door to eternal life with a loving God.

Jesus saves me from separation. Sin broke humankind into hostile fragments. Pain and hatred separate races, nations, classes, and even families and spouses. Through his church Jesus gathers believers into a new family that gets along, bound together by a common Father.

Jesus saves me from a useless existence. Sin made our lives totally useless. Nothing we did to try to save ourselves had a ghost of a chance of success. Our certain doom wiped out any enduring purpose to our lives. But Jesus gives our lives new meaning. He allows us to contribute to his eternal kingdom by telling the world about him.

The Church Says

> He has fully paid for all my sins with his precious blood,
> and has set me free from the tyranny of the devil.
> He also watches over me in such a way
> that not a hair can fall from my head
> without the will of my Father in heaven:
> in fact, all things must work together for my salvation.
>
> . . . [He] assures me of eternal life
> and makes me wholeheartedly willing and ready
> from now on to live for Him.
>
> (*Heidelberg Catechism A. 1*)

Hotseat Question

How can you be sure Jesus is *your* Savior?

Check It Out

John 11:21–27; 1 Peter 1:17–21; 1 John 3:1–10

| QUEST **13** | Why is he your *only* Savior? |

We Christians would get along much better with others if we dropped our claim that Jesus is the only *Savior of the world. Why not play footsie with Hindus, Humanists, and New Agers—all of whom believe that we can find our way back to God through* many *different paths? Jesus clearly rejects this "simple" solution. "I am the way and the truth and the life," he tells us. "No one comes to the Father except through me" (John 14:6).*

Some Possible Answers

Because I cannot save myself. Most religions teach that we can save ourselves by meditation, good works, or other achievements. The Bible explodes this myth. Anything we do to gain our own salvation is too little, too late. We cannot crawl back to God on our own. He must reach down to bring us back to himself.

Because only Jesus comes from the Father. Regardless of their boasts, all other religious leaders are only sinful people who need God to save them as much as we do. Only Jesus came from heaven to bridge the gulf between God and us. He warns: "All who ever came before me were thieves and robbers, but the sheep did not listen to them. I am the gate; whoever enters through me will be saved" (John 10:89).

Because only God can bear the punishment I deserve. No one except Jesus could ever shoulder the awful punishment our sins deserve. Only his divine power made him able to endure it for us all.

Because he alone is sinless. No one descended from Adam and Eve escapes the rot of sin. We inherit it from them like a genetic disease. Our sins disqualify even the best of us from saving others because we cannot even save ourselves. God had to break through the hopeless chain of human failure. Only the One conceived by the Holy Spirit, born of the virgin Mary could break it. He alone stands as the spotless Lamb of God who alone is worthy to take our place.

Because God will not let other creatures pay for my sins. God's justice demands that only a human representative can stand in our place. Animal sacrifices never paid for sin. Like a check, they only held out the promise of real payment at some future time. In all fairness, only someone who was really one of us could shoulder our punishment. Only the blood of Jesus would do.

He's all I need. Paul writes: "For God was pleased to have all his fullness dwell in him, and through him to reconcile to himself all things" (Col.1:19–20). Jesus is our One and only.

The Church Says

Can we pay this debt ourselves?

Certainly not.
Actually, we increase our guilt every day.

(Heidelberg Catechism Q. & A. 13)

**Can another creature—any at all—
pay this debt for us?**

No.
To begin with,
   God will not punish another creature
   for what a human is guilty of.
Besides,
   no mere creature can bear the weight
   of God's eternal anger against sin
   and release others from it.

(Heidelberg Catechism Q. & A. 14)

Hotseat Question

If you reject other faiths, are you narrow-minded?

Check It Out

John 14:1–6; Hebrews 2:14–18; Hebrews 7:22–28

QUEST
14

Why do you call Jesus "Christ"?

No doubt you know that "Christ" is not Jesus' surname. We do not attach this title just to distinguish him from other people called Jesus. To call him "Christ" means that we confess something important about him. This question asks you to be specific: what are you saying about Jesus when you call him "Christ"?

Some Possible Answers

Jesus is appointed by God himself. The term *Christ* means "anointed." In biblical times, officebearers had fragrant oil poured over their heads at their ordination. This anointing indicated that God equipped them for their task by pouring his Spirit on them. Jesus received that anointing at his baptism. To assure us that Jesus indeed is the Father's chosen One, God spoke from heaven: "This is my Son, whom I love; with him I am well pleased" (Matt. 3:17).

Jesus is my prophet. Like all true prophets, Jesus tells us what God has to say to us. Unlike the others, Jesus reveals *all* that God has to say to us. We should not look for any further prophecy beyond what he has taught us.

   Through the ages Jesus communicates God's truth by means of the Bible, which testifies of him. Christ is the last and the lasting Word of God. John writes: "No one has ever seen God, but God the One and Only, who is at the Father's side, has made him known" (John 1:18).

Jesus is my high priest. Like all true priests, Jesus approaches a holy God on behalf of his sinful people. He brings sacrifices to give thanks to God and to atone for sin. Unlike other priests, Jesus sacrificed *himself* for us. Since animal offerings could not remove our guilt, Jesus made the sacrifice that he alone could. His one gift on the cross covers all our sins for all time.

Jesus is my king. A king rules. But when a rebel tries to wrench away his power, he fights. So Jesus, our eternal king, battles Satan for control over us and our world. In his exaltation Jesus has begun to assert his rule. Though the fight remains fearfully cruel, we rest secure in the knowledge that on Calvary Jesus already struck the fatal blow. The battle continues to rage, but our king has already won the war. His rule will spread from our hearts to our lives, and from believers to the whole world.

Jesus remains in charge forever. All other officebearers held their offices only temporarily. They had a nasty habit of dying. In contrast, Jesus' term in office never ends. By appointing his Son to office, God ends the checkered cycle of good and bad leaders.

The Church Says

Because he has been ordained by God the Father
and has been anointed with the Holy Spirit
  to be
  our chief prophet and teacher
    who perfectly reveals to us
    the secret council and will of God for our deliverance;
  our only high priest
    who has set us free by the one sacrifice of his body,
    and who continually pleads our cause with the Father;
  and our eternal king
    who governs us by his Word and Spirit,
    and who guards us and keeps us
    in the freedom he has won for us.

                              (*Heidelberg Catechism A. 31*)

Hotseat Question

How do you experience Jesus' leadership in your life?

Check It Out

Matthew 3:13–17, 21:1–5; Luke 4:14–21; Hebrews 5:1–6

| QUEST 15 | Why do you call yourself a *Christian*? | *We cannot just attach the label "Christian" to anyone who forgoes alcohol, helps Aunt Sophie across the street, or stays honest at tax time. The proper use of the term challenges us to much more than honest and upright living.* |

Some Possible Answers

I share in Christ. Paul writes, "In Christ we who are many form one body, and each member belongs to all the others. We have different gifts, according to the grace given us" (Rom. 12:5–6). He goes on to list some of the gifts with which Christ entrusts us and tells us to use them zealously for the enrichment of all.

We expect our arms and legs to work for the good of our whole body, not to carry on a life of their own. Christ expects the same of us. *Christ*ians are the hands and feet of Jesus in this world; through us, he continues his redeeming work.

I share Christ's calling. Jesus is named "Christ" because he receives his task from God. As *Christians* we share his calling. Paul emphasizes this fact so strongly that in the original Greek he repeats the word *call* three times in one sentence: "I *call* on you to live a life worthy of the *calling* to which you have been *called* (Eph. 4:1). Our word *church* stems from the same word: *ekklesia*, which means "called-out ones." Jesus invites every Christian to share the task the Father has given to him: to reconcile the world to God.

I share Christ's prophetic task. Jesus does not require us to drum up a lot of new, innovative stuff—only to relay to others what he shows us of God's great love and work. We may share that good word with those who will die eternally without it.

I share Christ's priestly task. Because he sacrificed his life for us, Jesus asks us to sacrifice ours also. He asks us to give our money, our time, and our energy to benefit his kingdom. Sometimes he asks us for bigger sacrifices as well; we may be required to give up relationships, good times, freedom, or life itself. He also asks us to bring the needs of others before God's throne. By acting as priests, we extend the benefits of Christ's sacrifice to a deeply troubled world.

I share Christ's kingly task. We must fight the good fight until Christ returns to fully restore his kingdom. He asks us to handle wisely the authority he gives us over children, workers, students, citizens, and the earth. We must use our authority to advance his kingdom, not our own. Then, when he returns, we shall reign with him over the new creation.

The Church Says

> Because by faith I am a member of Christ
> and so I share in his anointing.
>   I am anointed
>   to confess his name,
>   to present myself to him as a living sacrifice of thanks,
>   to strive with a good conscious against sin and the devil
>   in this life,
>   and afterward to reign with Christ
>   over all creation
>   for all eternity.

(Heidelberg Catechism A. 32)

Hotseat Question

What do you see as your life's calling? Is it worthy of the name "Christian"?

Check It Out

Acts 2:14–24; 2 Timothy 2: 8–13; Hebrews 9:11–14

| QUEST **16** | How do you respond to Jesus' suffering? | *If you dwell too much on Jesus' suffering, you might respond inappropriately to it: you might pity him. The One who sits at God's right hand in glory certainly does not need your pity. You need his! You cannot and need not begin to know the depth of his agony. Yet, if you truly belong to him, the suffering of your Brother and best Friend must make a deep impact on your life.* |

Some Possible Answers

I'm horrified. When we look at the hellish agony Jesus suffered, we discover how bad our sins really are. We see how deeply we have hurt God. We also see how sin has ruined our human nature. We're faced squarely with sin's consequences. How utterly shocking what we did to the Son of God! Golgotha holds a mirror up to us so we clearly see how desperately we need God's help.

I'm relieved. When we see how Jesus suffered, we know that we will never need to face the same. He fully paid the debt. He set us free. As Isaiah promised:

> Surely he took up our infirmities
> and carried our sorrows,
> yet we considered him stricken by God,
> smitten by him, and afflicted.
> But he was pierced for our transgressions,
> he was crushed for our iniquities;
> the punishment that brought us peace was upon him,
> and by his wounds we are healed.
>
> (Isaiah 53:4–5)

It makes me very thankful. Jesus willingly took the punishment we deserve. How can we ever thank him enough? As one ancient hymn puts it:

> What language shall I borrow to thank you, dearest Friend,
> for this, your dying sorrow, your mercy without end?
> Lord, make me yours forever, a loyal servant true,
> and let me never, never outlive my love for you.
>
> (*"O Sacred Head, Now Wounded," stanza 3*)

It inspires me to serve him. Through his suffering Jesus binds us to himself. He is the Good Shepherd who gave his life for his sheep. Jesus clearly showed us why we should serve him rather than the devil, ourselves, or anyone else. He proved his love for us. He alone deserves our wholehearted commitment.

It makes me willing to accept suffering and make sacrifices. Jesus said: "If anyone would come after me, he must deny himself and take up his cross daily and follow me" (Luke 9:23). Suffering did not destroy Jesus, and it will not destroy us. Jesus obediently endured all that the world, the devil, and even the Father himself threw at him. He kept His eye on the goal. So may we: "We are heirs of God and co-heirs with Christ, if indeed we share in his sufferings in order that we may also share in his glory" (Rom. 8:17).

The Church Says

> **What further advantage do we receive**
> **from Christ's sacrifice and death on the cross?**
>
> Through Christ's death
> our old selves are crucified, put to death, and buried with him,
> so that the evil desires of the flesh
>   may no longer rule us,
> but that instead we may dedicate ourselves
>   as an offering of gratitude to him.
>
> *(Heidelberg Catechism Q. & A. 43)*

Hotseat Question

Can you give an example in your life of where you have "suffered with Christ"?

Check It Out

Matthew 16:21–28; Romans 6:1–14; Philippians 2:5–13

QUEST
17

What does the exaltation of Jesus mean to you?

Jesus did not remain in the grave. He rose from the dead, ascended into heaven, and sits at God's right hand. "Good for him!" we say. And we mean it. But we may have no idea what difference that makes to us. Christ's exaltation is crucial for Christians. Jesus not only died for us, he also lives for us. Our lives may not just go on as if he still lies in that tomb.

Some Possible Answers

It proves that he paid my sins in full. Suppose Jesus only managed to make partial payment for our sins. We would still have to make up the difference. To some extent we would have to earn our own salvation. Jesus' exaltation proves that that's not necessary. God loaded Jesus with the *full* burden of our sins. If that burden was too heavy for him, he would never have made it past the grave. He would not have risen. He would have remained in the hell of God's abandonment. But his exaltation proves that he *did* come through it. He fully cleared our God-account.

He conquered the grave for me. The world tells us that resurrections cannot happen. Jesus proved they can. After the crucifixion he was stone-cold dead. Just a few days later he bodily walked out of his grave.

When we or our loved ones face that bitter, final enemy, we know it will not defeat us. Jesus turns death into victory. Paul writes: "But Christ has indeed been raised from the dead, the firstfruits of those who have fallen asleep. For since death came through a man, the resurrection of the dead comes also through a man. For as in Adam all die, so in Christ all will be made alive" (1 Cor. 15:20–22).

I have a Mediator with God. As our high priest Jesus continues night and day to plead our cause before the Father. He bends God's ear for needs we do not even know we have. He covers even the sins we dare not admit to ourselves.

It assures me that I'm headed for heaven. Many hold the silly notion that heaven is filled with airy, harp-strumming souls floating around on puffy clouds. Jesus shows us otherwise. He bodily ascended into heaven: flesh, blood, bones, and all. "We have our own flesh in heaven—a guarantee that Christ our head will take us, his members, to himself in heaven" (Heidelberg Catechism A. 49).

I have a living king. Jesus did not leave us to fend for ourselves. "God placed all things under his feet and appointed him to be head over everything for the church, which is his body" (Eph. 1:22–23). Our risen Savior walks with us every step of the way.

The Church Says

> In all my distress and persecution
> I turn my eyes to the heavens
> and confidently await as judge the very One
>   who has already stood trial in my place before God
>   and so has removed the whole curse from me.
> All his enemies and mine
>   he will condemn to everlasting punishment:
> but me and all his chosen ones
>   he will take along with him
>   into the joy and the glory of heaven.
>
> (*Heidelberg Catechism* A. 52)

Hotseat Question

Where in your life did you really see that you share in Christ's victory?

Check It Out

Isaiah 9:1–7; 1 Corinthians 15:12–28; Revelation 1:12–18

| QUEST **18** | Why do you call Jesus your Lord? | *When we confess Jesus as Lord, we speak a real mouthful: We deny that he is only a death-insurance policy that we file away in the back of our minds until we need him. We agree that we cannot go on living as if nothing has changed. We state that he is more to us than just a Savior. But what?* |

Some Possible Answers

I belong to him. Today most people want to be independent. They want to control their own life and remain masters of their own destiny. Yet the catechism dares to declare that our only enduring comfort in life and death is this: "That I am not my own, but belong—body and soul, in life and in death—to my faithful Savior Jesus Christ" (Heidelberg Catechism A. 1).

As long as we live for ourselves, we're orphans. We wander through life lost, facing certain destruction. But when we belong to Jesus, we no longer stand alone. He gathers us into the family of God. Scripture tells us we don't have to go it alone. We have a Bridegroom who belongs to us as we belong to him. We're bound to him in a love relationship that will never go stale.

I obey him. When we recognize Jesus as our Lord, we place our lives under new management: his. We surrender our lives to his command. Jesus promises, "If you obey my commands, you will remain in my love. . . . I have told you this so that my joy may be in you and that your joy may be complete" (John 15:10–11). Unless we follow the way of our Master every day, we shipwreck our lives on our own shortsighted incompetence.

I live for him. Nothing is more shallow and empty than a life lived for its own sake. Being selfish will never make us happy. Only when we surrender our lives to our risen Lord will they take on real meaning and purpose. He alone can make sense of all our joys, sorrows, victories, and defeats. If we let him, he will fit all the bits and pieces of our lives together into a masterpiece of praise to God. "For we are God's workmanship, created in Christ Jesus to do good works, which God prepared in advance for us to do" (Eph. 2:10).

I trust him. Jesus is not only *our* Lord. God has made him Lord of the whole universe. Nothing, not even death, can stand in his way. Because he rules everything, I dare to put my whole life, in this world and the next, in his hands. No one else deserves such confidence.

The Church Says

Why do you call him "our Lord"?

Because—
    not with gold or silver,
    but with his precious blood—
he has set us free
    from sin and from the tyranny of the devil,
and has bought us,
    body and soul,
to be his very own.

(Heidelberg Catechism Q. & A. 34)

Hotseat Question

In which part of your life do you still rebel against Jesus' lordship?

Check It Out

Acts 2:29–36; Ephesians 1:15–23; Colossians 1:9–14

| QUEST **19** | Where do you meet Jesus in your life? | *When he ascended bodily into heaven, Jesus left us with more than memories. He clearly promised to remain with us. The question is how and where. If Jesus is physically in heaven, how can you really meet him here on earth? Where do you experience the risen Christ in Spirit, if not yet in body?* |

Some Possible Answers

In church. The Spirit of Christ does not float around empty church buildings. It is the people inside the buildings that provide unity with our risen Lord. Wherever believers meet, Jesus joins their fellowship. He promised, "Where two or three come together in my name, there am I with them" (Matt. 18:20).

In the Lord's Supper. Through our celebration of his supper, Jesus himself meets us. He is there—not physically in bread and wine, but not just in memory either. Through his Holy Spirit, Jesus presents himself as our host. He grants us his rich grace. He feeds us with the benefits of the sacrifice he made on the cross so long ago. We gratefully accept his amazing, unique offer: "Take and eat; this is my body" (Matt. 26:26).

In his Word. Through the reading and preaching of his Word, Jesus speaks to us daily. When we listen in faith, he reaches out to us across the centuries. Through the power of his Spirit, he talks not just to Tom, Dick, or Mary. He addresses us personally—one on one. That is why the Bible remains always relevant: "He calls his own sheep by name and leads them out . . . and his sheep follow him because they know his voice" (John 10:3–4).

In the eyes of those who need me. The exalted Lord so closely identifies with his followers that he suffers and celebrates what they experience. When we deal with Christians, we deal with Christ himself: "I tell you the truth, whatever you did for one of the least of these brothers of mine, you did for me" (Matt. 25:40).

In the task he gives me to do. Just before he ascended, Jesus reassured us: "Therefore, go and make disciples of all nations, baptizing them in the name of the Father and of the Son and of the Holy Spirit, and teaching them to obey everything I have commanded you. And surely I am with you always, to the very end of the age" (Matt. 28:19–20).

In my heart. Jesus promised he would dwell in us through his Spirit: "If you love me, you will obey what I command. And I will ask the Father, and he will give you another Counselor to be with you forever—the Spirit of truth. . . . I will not leave you as orphans; I will come to you. . . . On that day you will realize that I am in my Father, and you are in me, and I am in you" (John 14:15–20).

The Church Says

> **But isn't Christ with us**
> **until the end of the world**
> **as he promised us?**

> Christ is truly human and truly God.
>> In his human nature Christ is not now on earth;
>> but in his divinity, majesty, grace, and Spirit
>> he is not absent from us for a moment.
>
> *(Heidelberg Catechism Q. & A. 47)*

Hotseat Question

When in your life did you most strongly experience Jesus' presence?

Check It Out

John 14:15–31

| QUEST **20** | What do you expect Jesus to do for you in the future? |

What do you think of someone who becomes your friend for what they can get out of the relationship? Not much. In the same way, we shouldn't call Jesus "our Lord" just to get future benefits. But that doesn't mean we have to ignore those benefits. We can and should find comfort in Jesus' promises to stay with us until the end of the age (Matt. 28:20) and to bring us to live with him eternally.

Some Possible Answers

Protect me. Jesus does not guarantee us an easy cruise through life. He will not shelter us from every tragedy or hardship. But he has promised to bring us safely back to our Father's home. "For I am convinced that neither death nor life, neither angels nor demons, neither the present nor the future, nor any powers, neither height nor depth, nor anything else in all creation, will be able to separate us from the love of God that is in Christ Jesus our Lord (Rom. 8:38–39).

Give me eternal life. Jesus promises: "I am the resurrection and the life. He who believes in me will live, even though he dies; and whoever lives and believes in me will never die" (John 11:25).

Help me do my task in his kingdom. The risen Christ showers us with his kindness. He has given each of us gifts that we can use to build his kingdom. He creates opportunities to use those gifts. He could do it all himself. But Jesus gives purpose to our lives. What we do down here, he will take up into eternity.

Return to judge the world. On judgment day Jesus will return on the clouds of heaven. He will not come to embarrass us by dragging our dirty thoughts and deeds out into the open for everyone to see. He will not come to condemn us. Our judge will be our own lawyer! We have nothing to fear. On judgment day he will make public what we already know deep within our hearts: his blood has washed us clean. We stand fully pardoned before our God. "The Son of Man will send out his angels, and they will weed out of his kingdom everything that causes sin and all who do evil . . . . Then the righteous will shine like the sun in the kindom of their Father" (Matt. 13:41–43).

Give me my share in the New Jerusalem. Jesus promised: "In my Father's house are many rooms; . . . I am going to prepare a place for you" (John 14: 2). Brought up as a carpenter, Jesus was well equipped to do some building. But he made room for us with the Father not by using a hammer and nails but by dying on the cross. By healing our relationship to the Father, Jesus made us welcome once again in our Father's house. We already begin to enjoy that bond of fellowship with him today. But Jesus alone can establish the city in which we shall daily rub shoulders with our God. That's why the New Jerusalem comes down from heaven. It's not something we achieve. It's his wedding gift to us.

The Church Says

How does Christ's return
"to judge the living and the dead"
comfort you?

In all my distress and persecution
I turn my eyes to the heavens
and confidently await as judge the very One
    who has already stood trial in my place before God
    and so has removed the whole curse from me.
All his enemies and mine
    he will condemn to everlasting punishment:
but me and all his chosen ones
    he will take along with him
    into the joy and the glory of heaven.

(*Heidelberg Catechism Q. & A. 52*)

Hotseat Question

What's your deepest longing? Does Jesus play a part in filling it?

Check It Out:

Romans 8:31–39; 1 Thessalonians 4:13–18; Revelation 21

Rescued for Good

(Quests 21–30)

<table>
<tr><td>

QUEST

21

</td><td>

What makes you right with God?

</td><td>

Many people rightly see this as the most important question in the world. But their answer to it is dead wrong. They imagine their own good works will put them right with God. They try to gain salvation by jumping through a set of hoops they themselves construct.

The Bible gives us the answer to this question, an answer so surprising that we would never come up with it on our own. It's an answer that's important to know, to remember, and to share with those who ask the right question but need someone to help them find the right answer.

</td></tr>
</table>

Some Possible Answers

Nothing I can do. The Bible insists that our good works cannot make us right with God. We cannot pull ourselves up to heaven by our own bootstraps. We need to rely totally on what someone else has done for us. That bitter pill often makes us choke. As a result we waste our time finding ways of contributing to what has already been done for us. In the process we forget to give the only proper response: thanks! As one well-known hymn reminds us:

> Not what my hands have done can save my guilty soul;
> not what my toiling flesh has borne can make my spirit whole.
> Not what I feel or do can give me peace with God;
> not all my prayers and sighs and tears can bear my awful load.

What Christ has done for me. Jesus insists: "I am the way and the truth and the life. No one comes to the Father except through me" (John 14:6). He makes us right with God because he shoulders the full burden of our sin. He also fulfills for us all God's expectations. Bonar's hymn continues:

> Your voice alone, O Lord, can speak to me of grace;
> your power alone, O Son of God, can all my sin erase.
> No other work but yours, no other blood will do;
> no strength but that which is divine can bear me safely through.

By faith. Faith also is not our work but God's gift to us. It is the receiver by which we tune in to Christ's saving work. Paul writes: "Therefore, since we have been justified through faith, we have peace with God through our Lord

Jesus Christ, through whom we have gained access by faith into this grace in which we now stand" (Rom. 5:1–2).

By means of this saving faith we stop trying to accomplish our own salvation. We accept God's renewing work in our lives. Bonar's hymn concludes:

> I praise the Christ of God; I rest on love divine;
> and with unfaltering lip and heart I call this Savior mine.
> My Lord has saved my life and freely pardon gives;
> I love because he first loved me, I live because he lives.

The Church Says

How are you right with God?

Only by true faith in Jesus Christ.

> Even though my conscience accuses me
>   of having grievously sinned against all God's commandments
>   and of never having kept any of them,
> and even though I am still inclined toward all evil,
> nevertheless,
>   without my deserving it at all,
>   out of sheer grace,
> God grants and credits to me
> the perfect satisfaction, righteousness, and holiness of Christ,
>   as if I had never sinned nor been a sinner,
>   as if I had never been as perfectly obedient
>   as Christ was obedient for me.

> All I need to do
> is to accept this gift of God with a believing heart.
>   (*Heidelberg Catechism Q. & A. 60*)

Hotseat Question

In what ways have you tried to put yourself into God's good graces?

Check It Out

Acts 10:34–48; Romans 3:21–31

<table>
<tr><td>

QUEST

22

</td><td>

What does the Holy Spirit do for you?

</td><td>

Because the Holy Spirit points away from himself to Christ, we could easily overlook the crucial role he plays in our lives. This question asks us to identify some ways we experience his vital, saving work.

</td></tr>
</table>

Some Possible Answers

He's my link to Christ. Like power lines transmit electrical energy from the generator station to our homes, so the Holy Spirit applies the benefits of Jesus' saving work to us. By living in our hearts, the Spirit unites us with the risen, ascended Christ. Jesus promised: "I will ask the Father, and he will give you another Counselor to be with you forever—the Spirit of truth. . . . I will not leave you as orphans; I will come to you" (John 14:16–18).

He fully assures me that I'm God's child. Paul says: "For you did not receive a spirit that makes you a slave again to fear, but you received the Spirit of sonship. And by him we cry, '*Abba*, Father.' The Spirit himself testifies with our spirit that we are God's children" (Rom. 8:15–16).

He gives me saving faith. Even with the best of intentions we cannot choose to believe the Bible. We can come to saving faith in Christ only through the Spirit's convicting power. He must melt our rock-hard hearts into hearts of flesh. He must perform in us the miracle of rebirth: "I tell you the truth, no one can see the kingdom of God unless he is born again . . . no one can enter the kingdom of God unless he is born of water and the Spirit" (John 3:3–5).

He sanctifies me. Already in this life the Holy Spirit begins to purify us. He replaces our selfishness with the love of Christ. He replaces our despair with hope and our unbelief with true faith. He gives us gentleness, kindness, patience, and forgiveness. He makes us nail our old selves to Christ's cross and helps us walk in his footsteps. He makes us hate evil and love the good. One day he will remove completely our old nature and perfect the new. As the life-giver, he will remove all suffering, sin, and evil from us. He will fully make us what we already are in Christ: saints.

He makes me a living member of Christ's Church. Through all his gifts, and with love as the glue, the Holy Spirit molds us together into the new people of God. We do not remain individuals who stay separate and aloof from one another. Through the bond of love, the Spirit makes us share the resources he provides. We now work for the good of the whole body of Christ. By making us interdependent the Spirit makes us the everlasting, close-knit family of God.

The Church Says

**What do you believe
concerning "the Holy Spirit"?**

First, he, as well as the Father and the Son,
is eternal God.

Second, he has been given to me personally,
so that, by true faith,
he makes me share in Christ and all his blessings,
comforts me,
and remains with me forever.

(Heidelberg Catechism Q. & A. 53)

Hotseat Question

Where in your life do you most strongly resist the work of the Spirit? Why?

Check It Out

John 15:12–15; Acts 2:1–21; Galatians 5:13–26

| QUEST **23** | How do you know you're a born-again Christian? |

Many believers run into trouble when asked if they're born again. Because that phrase has been interpreted in a variety of ways, people are confused by it. To some it implies a special relationship to God that "average" Christians do not have. Others mean by it a specific, dramatic spiritual experience that a person can later point to. But the Bible uses the phrase "born again" to identify all true Christians. God's Word does not allow us to divide Christians into first-class and economy-fare types. "No one can see the kingdom of God unless he is born again" (John 3:3). There's no such thing as a Christian who has not been born again.

Some Possible Answers

I believe in Jesus. We cannot achieve saving faith on our own. It is a gift of God's Holy Spirit: "For it is by grace you have been saved, through faith—and this not from yourselves, it is the gift of God" (Eph. 2:8). Therefore, the fact that we believe proves that the Holy Spirit has given us rebirth.

Our physical birth was not something we ourselves planned or to which we knowingly contributed. In the same way our rebirth is God's gift by which he grants us saving faith in Christ. Regardless of how many or how few our God-given gifts, the gift of faith provides all the evidence we need that we are born again.

I'm alive in Christ. We do not need to know the exact time of our birth to know we were born. The fact that we walk and talk and breathe provides sufficient evidence of that. Similarly, the fact that we love the Lord and serve him offers ample proof that we are born again—even if we cannot point to a specific time in our lives when our rebirth took place. When we're alive in Christ, we may safely assume we are (re)born.

I've changed. As Christians we often look only at our faults and failures. We do that because we want to be humble. However, we need also to look at the good we do—not to become boastful but to honestly assess what God has been doing to us and through us. We may find ourselves giving up things we know God doesn't like. We may find ourselves doing things out of real love for God and our neighbor.

Such change would be impossible on our own. Someone else is working in us. Someone is molding us into new people. With thankfulness in our hearts we see the evidence of our own rebirth: "For we are God's workmanship, created in Christ Jesus to do good works, which God prepared in advance for us to do" (Eph. 2:10).

The Church Says

Are we so corrupt
that we are totally unable to do any good
and inclined toward all evil?

Yes, unless we are born again,
by the Spirit of God.

(Heidelberg Catechism Q. & A. 8)

What is the coming-to-life of the new self?

It is wholehearted joy in God through Christ
and a delight to do every kind of good
    as God wants us to.

(Heidelberg Catechism Q. & A. 90)

Hotseat Question

Is rebirth the end or the beginning of your spiritual journey?

Check It Out

John 3:1–21; Ephesians 2:1–10; 1 Peter 1:22–25

<table>
<tr><td>QUEST
24</td><td>What is the
saving faith
that God's
Spirit gives
you?</td><td>*Faith forms the essential link between us
and our Lord. Without it eternal life is
nothing more than a pious illusion for
us. How do we know we have this faith?
How do we know that what we have is
the real thing? This question asks us to
identify some of the components of faith.*</td></tr>
</table>

Some Possible Answers

Certain knowledge. Faith is a matter of the head. Hebrews calls it "being sure of what we hope for and certain of what we do not see" (Heb. 11:1). Like a compass, faith guides us to our destination.

The magnetic North Pole is invisible. We cannot see it. Yet the compass lets us know exactly where it is, unerringly guiding us to our destination through thick darkness and blinding storm.

In the same way faith guides us through life by pointing to what we cannot yet see: God, his kingdom, and his great salvation for us. By letting us grasp the teachings of God's Word, faith guides us safely home.

Unshakable trust. Faith is a matter of the heart. It not only lets us know the great things God does but assures us that he does them for us personally.

Faith forges a deep bond of love between God and us. As we experience that close relationship to him, we find ourselves secure in his love, regardless of what life may throw at us.

Faith keeps us firmly anchored in Christ. As the psalmist discovered: "Those who trust in the Lord are like Mount Zion, which cannot be shaken but endures forever" (Ps. 125:1).

Full-bodied commitment. Faith is a matter of the hands. It inspires us to act on what we know and feel about God.

By faith our hearts begin to beat as one with our Lord's. We become his saving, redeeming hands in this pain-filled world. In his name, we heal, we bless, we teach, and we guide. Jesus said: "I am the vine; you are the branches. If a man remains in me and I in him, he will bear much fruit; apart from me you can do nothing" (John 15:5). Faith incorporates us into Christ's work, as well as into his person.

All of the above. True faith is a matter of head, heart, and hands—of knowing, experiencing, and doing. Remove one of these and the triad of faith collapses into a useless, hollow shell. By giving us true faith the Holy Spirit makes us able to fulfill not only part of God's will, but all of it: "Love the Lord your God with *all your heart* and with *all your soul* and with *all your mind* and with *all your strength* (Mark 12:30).

The Church Says

What is true faith?

True faith is
   not only a knowledge and conviction
      that everything God reveals in his Word is true;
   it is also a deep-rooted assurance,
      created in me by the Holy Spirit through the gospel
      that, out of sheer grace earned for us by Christ,
         not only others, but I too,
            have had my sins forgiven,
            have been made forever right with God,
            and have been granted salvation.

(Heidelberg Catechism Q. & A. 21)

It is impossible
   for those grafted into Christ by true faith
   not to produce fruits of gratitude.

(Heidelberg Catechism A. 64)

Hotseat Question

In what area does your faith need to grow the most: knowing, feeling, or doing?

Check It Out

Hebrews 11:1–3ff.; Romans 4:18–25; Hebrews 4:14–16

Why did God choose you?

Millions of people in this world lived and died without coming to saving faith in Christ. Most never even got a chance to say yes or no to the gospel because it never reached them. We did. God gave us his Word and Spirit. He brought us into a living relationship with his Son. Why us?

Some Possible Answers

Not because I'm any better than others. The fact that God elected us might lead us to the arrogant assumption that we're somehow better than others and therefore more desirable to God. We might imagine ourselves more pious or more willing to believe than others. Or we might think our family or racial origins had something to do with our election.

However, the Bible clearly teaches that God did not choose us because he found us more desirable than others. Our election is unconditional. He chooses a cheater like Jacob, a prostitute like Rahab, and a foreigner like Ruth. Paul writes: "Like the rest, we were by nature objects of wrath. But because of his great love for us, God, who is rich in mercy, made us alive with Christ even when we were dead in transgressions—it is by grace you have been saved" (Eph. 2:3–5).

I could not choose him. If God did not choose us first, he'd have no children besides Jesus. No one in the whole world would return to God on his or her own. Stumbling in the darkness, no one could find the way. No one would even want to.

Therefore God takes the first step. He brings his saving work into our lives to make us willing and able to respond to him. As one hymn puts it:

> I sought the Lord, and afterward I knew
> he moved my soul to seek him, seeking me;
> it was not I that found, O Savior true;
> no, I was found, was found of thee.

He loves me. How can he marry a woman like that? How can that mother love such a homely, mean-spirited child? Love must be blind.

God's love must be blind too. Paul tells us that God loved us while we were yet sinners. He started with creatures who had nothing desirable about them. Infected and crippled by the rot of sin, we were repulsive to a holy, perfect God. But he loved us. No one knows how he could, but he did.

He chose us. He called us. He justified us. He freely gave us his only Son. And through that love he glorifies us. More and more we image Jesus in our lives. His love transforms us into creatures that become lovable—into real daughters and sons.

The Church Says

Election [or choosing] is God's unchangeable purpose by which he did the following:

Before the foundation of the world,

by sheer grace, according to the free good pleasure of his will, he chose in Christ to salvation a definite number of particular people out of the entire human race, which had fallen by its own fault from its original innocence into sin and ruin. Those chosen were neither better nor more deserving than the others, but lay with them in the common misery.

(Canons of Dort, Pt. I, Art. 7)

Hotseat Question

How can you be sure God has chosen you?

Check It Out

John 10:14–30; Romans 8:28–39; Ephesians 1:3–14

<table>
<tr><td>

QUEST

26
</td><td>

If you're saved by grace alone, why do you still need to do good?
</td><td>

We do not get to heaven because of our good works. But we will not get there without them either. As the song says:
  You can't get to heaven on a
    rockin' chair
  'Cause God don' want no lazy
    bones dere.
This question challenges us to explain the necessity of following Christ without minimizing in any way what he did for us.
</td></tr>
</table>

Some Possible Answers

I can't do anything else. Good works are the necessary effects of Christ's work in us, the fruit of our salvation. He takes us from the misery of our rebellion against God and reshapes us into his own likeness.

   If we do not see the effects of his almighty, recreating hand in our lives, we have a clear warning that we are still far from grace. For if we really are grafted into Christ, the good tree, we will produce good fruit—naturally.

To give thanks to God. When we see what God has done for us, thankfulness naturally wells up in us. We express that gratitude through our many acts of worship. But that's just the start. Like a glass filled to overflowing, our thankfulness spills over into our deeds, lives, and relationships. Not self-righteousness, but sheer joy-filled gratitude to our God energizes our lives. That's what really makes believers tick.

I see so much that still needs doing. God adopted us to be his children out of sheer grace, not because we deserved it in any way. But precisely because he made us his children through Christ, we begin to share his concern with those who are still lost. We want to take part in the family business of redeeming the world and reconciling it again to its Creator. Jesus said: "You are the light of the world . . . let your light shine before men, that they may see your good deeds and praise your Father in heaven" (Matt. 5:14–16).

I don't want to live any other way. After Christ has saved us from the slimy pit of sin and death, the last thing we want to do is crawl back into it. Instead, we want to exercise these limbs of faith as we try to walk in step with his Spirit. It helps us know we're really alive.

The Church Says

We have been delivered
from our misery
by God's grace alone through Christ
and not because we have earned it:
why then must we still do good?

To be sure, Christ has redeemed us by his blood.
But we do good because
    Christ by his Spirit is also renewing us to be like himself,
    so that in all our living
    we may show that we are thankful to God
        for all he has done for us,
    and so that he may be praised through us.

And we do good
    so that we may be assured of our faith by its fruits,
    and so that by our godly living
        our neighbors may be won over to Christ.

(Heidelberg Catechism Q. & A. 86)

Hotseat Question

Can you identify some of those good works in your life?

Check It Out

John 15:1–17; 1 Peter 2:4–12

How can you keep your faith growing?

If we don't use our faith, we lose it. When your parents gave you a pet, they expected you to care for it. So God expects us to responsibly nurture this living, breathing, vital gift of faith. Do we know how to do that and where to look? More importantly, perhaps, do we actually use the means he provides?

Some Possible Answers

By feeding it. In order to grow, our faith needs a constant diet of God's Word. We can feed on that Word in such a rich variety of ways that we only list a few of them:

1. listening carefully to sermons
2. celebrating the sacraments
3. participating actively in family devotions
4. reading the Bible
5. reading good Christian literature
6. participating in a Bible study or discussion group
7. taking church education courses *after* making public profession of faith

By exercising it. Like our muscles, faith grows strongest when we exercise it in many ways.

We need to exercise our faith in prayer. By holding God to his promises, we discover that he really does come through for us. That makes us grow.

We also need to exercise our faith in worship. In that communal celebration the Spirit strengthens us by welding us into a common bond of faith. In solidarity with each other we share in a dynamic conversation with our risen Lord.

We need to exercise our faith by making sacrifices. The more we dare to put Christ's kingdom ahead of our own, the more our will merges with his. By stepping out in faith to be God's servants, we become more and more dedicated to his marvelous mission in this world. We increasingly understand how the apostles could rejoice even in their sufferings: "The apostles left the Sanhedrin, rejoicing because they had been counted worthy of suffering disgrace for the Name [of Jesus]" (Acts 5:41).

By sharing it. A glowing cinder dies out quickly when it pops out of the fire. So our faith quickly cools when we separate ourselves from the body of Christ and from the means of his grace. We need to warm each other with the energy and vitality of our shared faith. In our fellowship Jesus himself meets us.

We also make our faith grow by giving it away. When we teach the good news, we learn more about it ourselves. When we witness to others, we ourselves gain strength and confidence in God's truth—even if those we witness to saunter off with a quizzical smirk.

The Church Says

It is by faith alone
that we share in Christ and all his blessings:
where then does that faith come from?

The Holy Spirit produces it in our hearts
    by the preaching of the holy gospel,
and confirms it
    through our use of the holy sacraments.

(Heidelberg Catechism Q. & A. 65)

Why do Christians need to pray?

Because prayer is the most important part
    of the thankfulness God requires of us.
And also because God gives his grace and Holy Spirit
only to those who pray continually and groan inwardly,
    asking God for these gifts
    and thanking him for them.

(Heidelberg Catechism Q. & A. 116)

Hotseat Question

Do you feed your faith a balanced diet?

Check It Out

Proverbs 3:1–8; Matthew 28:16–20; Hebrews 10:22–25

| QUEST 28 | What evidence of salvation do you find in your life? | *Some people experience such dramatic conversions that they can point to the exact minute. For others the realization of salvation creeps up gradually. In either case we need to be aware of the very real changes that God's salvation produces in our lives. These (re)assure us that we are in Christ and provide good reasons to thank God.* |

Some Possible Answers

Sin is losing its appeal. Our sin-twisted lives don't seem all that bad until we see them from the perspective of grace. We begin to see clearly how horrible sin and its consequences really are. Like a child learns to shun a cactus because of its thorns, we begin to hate sin because of the injury it causes God, ourselves, and each other.

I enjoy doing God's work. It really feels good to do good. Sometimes it's difficult and tedious. But it's worth it. Doing good helps us experience a unity with God—a unity that comes from working side by side as partners in this exciting, complicated, frustrating, exhilarating work of kingdom-building.

Doing good fills our lives with new purpose. Our successes and even our failures take on fresh meaning.

I'm learning to love God and my neighbor. The self-sacrificing love of Christ cuts through our small-minded selfishness to make us look beyond ourselves. We catch ourselves doing things for God not because we *have* to but because we *want* to. Because we know we are already saved, we no longer spend our time trying to claw our own way into heaven. We have a whole lifetime with nothing better to do than to show concern for the welfare of others. And the more we give away Christ's love, the more we receive it back again. That's really living!

I'm learning self-control. Some of us have been burdened with a short fuse, others with an over-inflated ego, and others still with a razor-sharp tongue. Those personality defects do not magically disappear when we are saved. However, God's Spirit helps us to manage and control them. Through the power of the risen Christ we gain the freedom to overcome our weaknesses as Christ lives in us.

God's Word is coming through loud and clear to me now. The more we feast on the living Bread, the more we understand it and hunger for it. Words that used to be shrouded in dark mystery now shine with new meaning and joy. We begin to discover not only how well we can understand God's Word but also how well it understands us. We find what the psalmist confessed: "Your word is a lamp to my feet and a light for my path" (Ps. 119:105).

The Church Says

**What is involved
in genuine repentance or conversion?**

Two things:
    the dying-away of the old self,
    and the coming-to-life of the new.

                            (Heidelberg Catechiism Q. & A. 88)

What is the dying-away of the old self?

It is to be genuinely sorry for sin,
to hate it more and more,
and to run away from it.

                            (Heidelberg Catechism Q. & A. 89)

What is the coming-to-life of the new self?

It is wholehearted joy in God through Christ
and a delight to do every kind of good
    as God wants us to.

                            (Heidelberg Catechism Q. & A. 90)

Hotseat Question

Which parts of your life still need to change?

Check It Out

Romans 6:1–14; 2 Corinthians 5:14–15; Galatians 2:19–21

QUEST 29

What do you expect from God in *this* life?

We dream more about what our salvation means for us in the life to come than in this life. Yet God promises us all sorts of things for now as well. What are they? As a Christian, what will your life on this earth be like? Can you list some of the things God's Word leads you to expect?

Some Possible Answers

Ice cream and bee stings. God never promised us success by earthly standards. We will not always get what we want, and very few of us will manage to laze through life on "flowery beds of ease." We should expect our share of headaches, heartaches, and tough times.

However, God does promise to give us what we need if we ask in faith. Jesus assures us: "If you, then, though you are evil, know how to give good gifts to your children, how much more will your Father in heaven give good gifts to those who ask him!" (Matt. 7:11).

Strength to endure. God promises that he will never give us burdens too heavy for us to carry. He will ask us to make big sacrifices. He will allow Satan to tempt us, hurt us, and persecute us. But he will also lend us the strength and stamina we need to measure up.

Christ consoles us: "Take my yoke upon you and learn from me, for I am gentle and humble in heart, and you will find rest for your souls. For my yoke is easy and my burden is light" (Matt. 11:28–30). The burden of his teaching is light not because it doesn't ask a lot from us. It does. He does not offer us "cheap grace." His burden is light only because he himself helps us to carry it.

Direction and guidance. God promises to show us the way through life if we look to him in faith. By the talents he gives us, the doors he opens and shuts, and the people he puts on our path, he shows us where we may best serve his kingdom. Especially through his Word he shepherds us on our way: "Your word is a lamp to my feet and a light for my path" (Ps. 119:105).

His unfailing love. Sometimes we may feel that God is far away from us. But that's just a feeling. Even if we've strayed far from him, he's never more than a heartbeat away. Paul assures us: "If we are faithless, he will remain faithful, for he cannot disown himself" (2 Tim. 2:13).

God will not stoop to our unfaithfulness. His love will hold us fast through thick and thin. Until our dying gasp, we will find his fatherly arms stretched out to us.

The power of his Spirit. Through the gift of faith God's Spirit will energize us even when we've run out of steam. He will fall afresh on us and rekindle that sacred flame that makes us burn ourselves out for the One he makes us love.

The Church Says

> I trust him so much that I do not doubt
>   he will provide
>   whatever I need
>   for body and soul,
>   and he will turn to my good
>   whatever adversity he sends me
>   in this sad world.

(Heidelberg Catechism A. 26)

Hotseat Question

Has God kept his promises to you so far? Explain.

Check It Out

Matthew 6:25–34; 10:28–39

QUEST 30	What's your hope for the life to come?

The portal of death swings only one way. Life's end sweeps us through it never to return. What's on the other side?

That question is crucial. If there is no life after death, we might as well make the most of this life, seeking all the selfish pleasures and joys we can squeeze into our three-score and ten. Sacrifices, self-denial, giving God a hand, building his kingdom—all these things are useless to us if death is the end.

If death is not the end, on the other hand, these same things become both useful and necessary. But how can we be sure? How do we know what to expect when we've drawn our final breath? Is our service to God really worth the effort? Nobody ever came back from the dead to tell us, right?

Wrong! Jesus did just that!

Some Possible Answers

I'll be with the Lord forever. "In my Father's house are many rooms; if it were not so, I would have told you. I am going there to prepare a place for you. And if I go and prepare a place for you, I will come back and take you to be with me that you also may be where I am" (John 14:2–3).

I'll be given a glorified body. "So will it be with the resurrection of the dead. The body that is sown is perishable, it is raised imperishable; it is sown in dishonor, it is raised in glory; it is sown in weakness, it is raised in power; it is sown a natural body, it is raised a spiritual body" (1 Cor. 15:42–44).

He'll wipe away every tear. "They will be his people, and God himself will be with them and be their God. He will wipe every tear from their eyes. There will be no more death or mourning or crying or pain, for the old order of things has passed away" (Rev. 21:3–4).

He'll reward the good I did and forgive the bad. "Then I heard a voice from heaven say, 'Write: Blessed are the dead who die in the Lord from now on.' 'Yes,' says the Spirit, 'they will rest from their labor, for their deeds will follow them' " (Rev. 14:13).

I'll be free from sin. "Dear friends, now we are children of God, and what we will be has not yet been made known. But we know that when he appears, we shall be like him, for we shall see him as he is. Everyone who has this hope in him purifies himself, just as he is pure" (1 John 3:2–3).

I'll live in perfect harmony with all God's people. "After this I looked and there before me was a great multitude that no one could count, from every nation, tribe, people and language, standing before the throne and in front of the Lamb . . . 'These are they who have come out of the great tribulation; they have washed their robes and made them white in the blood of the Lamb' " (Rev. 7:9,14).

The Church Says

Not only my soul
  will be taken immediately after this life
  to Christ its head,
but even my very flesh, raised by the power of Christ,
  will be reunited with my soul
  and made like Christ's glorious body.

(Heidelberg Catechism A. 57)

Even as I already now
  experience in my heart
  the beginning of eternal joy,
so after this life I will have
  perfect blessedness such as
    no eye has seen,
    no ear has heard,
    no human heart has ever imagined:
a blessedness in which to praise God eternally.

(Heidelberg Catechism A. 58)

Hotseat Question

Are you afraid to die?

Check It Out

1 Corinthians 15:35–58

Living Bread

(Quests 31–40)

QUEST	Why do you	*You can't believe everything you read,*
31	trust the	*especially in religious tracts! While they*
	Bible?	*usually pitch for your deepest*

Why do you trust the Bible?

You can't believe everything you read, especially in religious tracts! While they usually pitch for your deepest commitment, they often stand on the shakiest ground, making more ridiculous and outrageous claims than late-night T.V. commercials. Because the Bible asks you to entrust your heart and soul to its message, you have to be really sure it's not a fake. How do you know?

Some Possible Answers

Because it is God's Word. The apostle Paul confirms: "All Scripture is God-breathed and is useful for teaching, rebuking, correcting and training in righteousness, so that the man of God may be thoroughly equipped for every good work" (2 Tim. 3:16–17).

Peter insists that the Bible writers did not saddle us with cleverly devised fables that they sucked out of their thumb. Rather, "men spoke from God as they were carried along by the Holy Spirit" (2 Pet. 1:21).

Because the Spirit convinces me. We cannot argue ourselves into trusting the Bible. Either we do or we don't. We can show lots of evidence for its authenticity. We can prove its reliability in many instances. We can even demonstrate its amazing integrity as it spans many centuries. But ultimately we cannot talk ourselves into believing the Bible.

Only the Holy Spirit can open our eyes, minds, and hearts to recognize the truth of God's Word. As its prime Author he alone convinces us that this Word knows us better than we know ourselves. And as we carefully study the Scriptures, he empowers us to meet God in its pages, dispelling all our doubts.

Because it is infallible. The Bible is so completely reliable that it unfailingly steers us in the right direction. It deserves to fully guide our believing and our doing.

However, it demands that we read it faithfully, carefully, and responsibly. All too easily we miss the Bible's real intent by twisting its message. By riding our own hobby horses we place ourselves on slippery ground. We need to interpret the Bible according to its own God-inspired intent, not ours.

Because it tells what the eyewitnesses saw. The Bible marshals witness after witness through century after century. All of them tell the same story: God so loves us that he sent us his Son. He proved his love by the historical facts of the birth, death, and resurrection of Jesus the Messiah. The prophets foretold it. The apostles confirm it.

God firmly fixes the truth and reliability of Scripture on the bedrock of history. What the Bible proclaims actually happened. God's wondrous deeds convincingly demonstrate that his Word deserves our wholehearted trust.

What the Church Says

> And we believe
> without a doubt
> all things contained in [the books of Scripture]—
> not so much because the church
> receives and approves them as such
> but above all because the Holy Spirit
> testifies in our hearts
> that they are from God,
> and also because they
> prove themselves
> to be from God.
>
> For even the blind themselves are able to see
> that the things predicted in them do happen.
>
> *(Belgic Confession Article 5)*

Hotseat Question

Do you spend enough time with the Word? Why or why not?

Check It Out

John 16:5–16; 2 Timothy 3; 2 Peter 1:12–21

QUEST **32**	What good news does the Bible address to you?	*When we can't see the forest for the trees, we get lost. The same thing happens when we bury ourselves in the specific texts and details of God's Word without stepping back to view its over-arching message. We must read each part of the Bible in the context of the whole. Can you summarize the basic message God directs your way in his Word? What does he tell you? Your answer to that basic question will guide both your study of the Bible and your whole life.*

Some Possible Answers

Creation, fall, and redemption. In the beginning God created all things good. However, Adam and Eve plunged all creation, including us, into sin. But through his tremendous love God is restoring the world to himself. Through Christ he removes the guilt of our sin. Through his Spirit he cleanses us and restores creation's goodness. When Christ returns, he will gather all believers into the New Jerusalem. There we will live with him forever in glory.

God loves me so much he gave me his Son. God wrote us a love letter. We call it the Bible. In this letter he tells us how deeply he cares for us: "For God so loved the world that he gave his one and only Son, that whoever believes in him shall not perish but have eternal life. For God did not send his Son into the world to condemn the world, but to save the world through him" (John 3:16–17). God asks us to respond to his love by loving him back.

Christ. We find Jesus on every page of the Bible. We don't just artificially paste him in—he's really there. On the road to Emmaus, Jesus, "beginning with Moses and all the Prophets, explained to them what was said in all the Scriptures concerning himself" (Luke 24:27).

The Old Testament tells us why Jesus had to come and how God prepared the way for his entry into our world. The New Testament relates what he did to bring salvation and how he is working it out in our lives and in the world.

God renews his covenant with me. God promised to reward our obedience with his rich blessing. He also warned that our disobedience would bring his curse down on our heads. We disobeyed.

In his unimaginable goodness God provided his own dear Son to shoulder the curse we deserved. Through the blood of Jesus he renews his covenant with us. He extends new conditions, based now not on our works but on faith.

> If we died with him,
> we will also live with him;
> if we endure,
> we will also reign with him.
> If we disown him,
> he will also disown us;
> if we are faithless,
> he will remain faithful,
> for he cannot disown himself.

2 Timothy 2:11–13

The Church Says

> And this is God's gospel promise:
>> to forgive our sins and give us eternal life
>>> by grace alone
>>> because of Christ's one sacrifice
>>> finished on the cross.

(Heidelberg Catechism A. 66)

Hotseat Question

How does this basic message relate to your daily life?

Check It Out

Luke 24:13–35; Acts 2:36–39

<table>
<tr><td>

QUEST

33

</td><td>

Can you list
some rules
that might
help you
interpret
the Bible
rightly?

</td><td>

*Well-intentioned people twist the Bible to
make it say the silliest things. Some use it
to defend apartheid, others to excuse the
way they treat their wives. But true
obedience to Scripture forbids such
distortions. The Bible will only yield
truth if we discover its God-given intent.
Can you list some rules that might help
us do that?*

</td></tr>
</table>

Some Possible Answers

Interpret Scripture with Scripture. Taken out of context, any passage of the
Bible can mislead us. We may not chop the Bible up into little, unrelated
nuggets that we arrange and rearrange to suit our fancy. Instead, we should
note the interrelationships and links the Bible provides. These help us to
understand its parts. Too often we're done listening before the Bible is done
telling. That leaves us with nothing but half-truths—the worst lies of all.

Determine its setting. The more we fill in the historical and geographical
backdrop of a text, the more clearly it speaks to us. God used flesh and
blood people to reveal his Word. The more we know about them and their
place in salvation history, the better we can see him.

Determine the type of writing. The Bible uses many forms of communication:
narrative, poetry, parable, and proverb, and so on. We may not confuse one
type of writing with another. If we do, we get nonsense. Each has its own
way of communicating and of being understood.

Find out what it says about Christ. Jesus is the key to understanding the Good
News. As the Incarnate Word, he stands at its center. Old and New Testament
alike testify of him. We need to ask the following question of every text: How
does this passage lead me to Christ and help me follow him?

Pray for the Spirit's guidance. No method will ensure success in understanding
Scripture. Rules may help us avoid mistakes. But only the Holy Spirit can
truly open our hearts, minds, and lives to God's Word. He alone can make
us recognize and understand the voice of our Good Shepherd. Jesus
promised: "When he, the Spirit of truth, comes, he will guide you into all
truth. He will not speak on his own . . . . He will bring glory to me by taking
what is mine and making it known to you" (John 16:13–14).

Consult the findings of others. Jesus poured his Spirit out on the *community* of believers. Therefore, we need to share our insights into the truth. The meaning one person finds in a passage may be corrected or supplemented by another. By consulting the writings of saints far removed from us in time and space, we can share their insights.

The Church Says

God himself began to reveal the gospel already in Paradise;
later, he proclaimed it
   by the holy patriarchs and prophets,
and portrayed it
   by the sacrifices and other ceremonies of the law;
finally, he fulfilled it
   through his own dear Son.

(Heidelberg Catechism A. 19)

Hotseat Question

What do you do if you cannot understand what you read?

Check It Out

Acts 8:26–40

QUEST **34**	Do the results of science threaten your faith in the Bible? Explain.

Sometimes science seems to contradict the Bible—especially when we look at the origins of the universe or the findings of archeology. Some people consider the gap between the Bible and science so wide that they have given up on one or the other altogether. How about you? Do these difficulties concern you?

Some Possible Answers

No. When rightly understood the Bible and the creation will agree. Since God refuses to lie, he will not mislead us either in the Bible or in the creation record. Therefore, we can be sure the two would agree if we interpreted them correctly.

But we don't always do that. Biblical interpretation and science are both human works. Because we can make mistakes in either or both, we sometimes run into snags. Such seeming inconsistencies do not deny the truth of Scripture or the truth of science. They only indicate that we do not have the whole picture yet and that we humbly should keep searching for answers.

No. Because the Bible and creation speak of such different things, contradictions are unimportant. The Bible's subject matter is very different from that in a science textbook. Scripture reveals to us the relationship between God and his creation—particularly his covenant relationship with humankind. Science concerns itself with inter-relationships within the creation itself. It seeks to understand the ways in which God's laws operate within the universe.

These very different fields of interest overlap only slightly. The contradictions that surface between them remain trivial.

No. The results of science generally confirm Scripture. Archeology and other scientific disciplines cannot prove or deny the truth of Scripture. That far exceeds their area of competence. However, these disciplines do show that the historical data Scripture offers along the way turns out to be highly accurate. That tells us that Bible authors carefully recorded what really happened. But of course, as believers, we already knew that.

No. Science enhances my faith. We need not fear the results of responsible scientific work. Where it pinches, its results are always open to correction, expansion, and revision. Actually, many scientific discoveries help us understand the Bible better. They give us a deeper insight and appreciation of what the Bible tells us.

In that way God's creation Word enlightens our Bible study just as our Bible study illumines our study of creation. Faith knows how to make these two work hand in hand without causing undue friction or interference in either direction.

The Church Says

God's Spirit leads us into Truth,
    the Truth of Christ's salvation,
    into increasing knowledge of all existence.
      He rejoices in human awareness of God's creation,
      and gives freedom to those on the frontiers of research.
We are overwhelmed by the growth in our knowledge.
    While our truth comes in broken fragments,
    we expect the Spirit to unite these in Christ.

(Our Song of Hope, stanza 14)

Hotseat Question

Have you had doubts about the reliability of the Bible? If so, what did you do about them?

Check It Out

Job 38:1–7, 31–41; Psalm 8; 111:10; 1 Corinthians 2:6–16

QUEST **35**	**How do you regularly feed on God's Word?**

If your Bible only provides ballast for your bookshelf, it remains a book of dead letters. Only when you read it, study it, and live it will its message fill you with new life. You make a habit of eating to stay alive. Do you also routinely feed on God's Word? How?

Some Possible Answers

I attend church. Worship services provide us with the opportunity to dialogue communally with God's Word. In the reading and preaching of the Scriptures God speaks to us. We respond by singing, praying, and sharing. In this way God builds us up as his people, and we give him the glory he so richly deserves.

I join in family devotions. Family worship grounds, supports, and informs the communal worship of God's people. That's why we should practice it diligently. God asks families to do more: to model his ways as well. But faithful family Bible study, prayer, and singing provide the backbone of that larger task. Family devotions draw best the connections between God and daily life. Christian schools and communal Bible studies cannot replace this covenant obligation.

I have my own personal devotions. The more we mine the Scriptures, the more we realize how incredibly rich and deep the wisdom of God is. We may choose to simply read our way through the Bible, or we may want to supplement our reading with the reflections of others on the passage we're studying. Whatever works for us, regular time spent alone with the Word of God yields rich rewards.

I participate in a Bible-study group. A study group helps us dig into the Word by sharing its meaning with others. As we trade insights and float ideas, we experience the communion of saints.

However, such groups do require a common commitment to adequate preparation. The first law of computers applies also to small group meetings: "Garbage goes in; garbage comes out."

I participate in adult church-education classes. Increasingly, churches recognize the importance of educating the mature as well as the young. Public profession may not end our growth in faith-knowledge. Adult education classes help foster our continued spiritual development.

By sharing it with others. To really learn something, teach it. Nothing helps us master the truth of Scripture better than to share and model it. We can do that by joining in the teaching ministry of our church. The Word feeds us best when we feed others on it.

The Church Says

> As God's people hear the Word and do it,
> they are equipped for discipleship,
> to witness to the good news:
> Our world belongs to God
> and he loves it deeply.

(Our World Belongs to God, 36)

Hotseat Question

When does God's Word reach you most powerfully?

Check It Out

Isaiah 55; Acts 2:41–42; 2 Timothy 3:14–4:5

<table>
<tr><td>QUEST
36</td><td>**What does your baptism mean to you?**</td><td>*Maybe you're looking forward to being baptized upon making public profession of your faith. Or maybe you were baptized as a baby. In either case baptism carries the same meaning. When we make public profession we say that we accept the promises God makes to us in our baptism. To do that intelligently we need to know what they are.*</td></tr>
</table>

Some Possible Answers

I'm God's child. Nobles of old placed a seal on a letter to identify it as their own. Baptism is God's seal, demonstrating that we belong to him. Throughout our lives we may rest secure in the knowledge that we have a faithful heavenly Father who cares for us no matter what happens.

Baptism also reminds us that he expects us to behave like his children. The staggering price he paid to make us his own prohibits us from betraying his love.

I belong to God's people. Baptism is the sign of God's covenant renewal with us. Because of Christ's sacrifice God receives not only Jews but also Gentiles into his covenant community. Peter proclaims: "Repent and be baptized, every one of you . . . . The promise is for you and your children and for all who are far off—for all whom the Lord our God will call" (Acts 2:38–39).

Through baptism Jesus gathers us into his church. We become members of his body. Our baptism challenges us to be living members, not dead meat.

It reminds me of what Jesus did for me. The water of baptism symbolizes cleansing—the washing away of our sins by the blood of Christ. Just as really and surely as the water splashes on our forehead, Jesus washed away our guilt before God on Calvary's cross. In this way baptism reassures us that we are right with God. But it also challenges us to live as forgiven and cleansed people: "Don't you know that all of us who were baptized into Christ Jesus were baptized into his death? We were therefore buried with him through baptism into death in order that, just as Christ was raised from the dead through the glory of the Father, we too may live a new life" (Rom. 6:3–4).

I share in Christ and his Spirit. Baptism reminds us that Jesus bought us with his own precious blood. We belong to him as he belongs to us. By baptism God grafts us as branches into Jesus, the living vine. He also grants us his Spirit that we may be *living* branches. Peter promises "Repent and be baptized, every one of you, in the name of Jesus Christ for the forgiveness of your sins. And you will receive the gift of the Holy Spirit" (Acts 2:38).

Baptism challenges us to receive these gifts with a believing heart. As Jesus' new life surges through ours, we cannot fail to bear fruit in his kingdom.

The Church Says

**What does it mean
to be washed with Christ's blood and Spirit?**

To be washed with Christ's blood means
  that God, by grace, has forgiven my sins
    because of Christ's blood
    poured out for me in his sacrifice on the cross.

To be washed with Christ's Spirit means
  that the Holy Spirit has renewed me
  and set me apart to be a member of Christ
    so that more and more I become dead to sin
    and increasingly live a holy and blameless life.

(Heidelberg Catechism Q. & A. 70)

Hotseat Question

When in your life did the meaning of your baptism really hit home?

Check It Out

Ezekiel 36:24–27; Acts 2:38–39; Romans 6:1–14

<table>
<tr><td>

QUEST 37

</td><td>

What reasons can you give for the practice of baptizing infants?

</td><td>

All churches practice believers' baptism for converts who come from non-Christian homes. But they disagree sharply on the issue of infant baptism. Should children of believers be baptized before they are able to profess their faith? Neither side has been able to convince the other that Scripture unambiguously affirms their position. Nevertheless the Reformed tradition has unswervingly kept the practice of infant baptism and, we believe, for solid biblical reasons. Can you list some?

</td></tr>
</table>

Some Possible Answers

God includes children of believers in his covenant. In both Old and New Testaments God includes in his covenant the children of those he has called—in the Old Testament through circumcision and in the New Testament through baptism. Peter affirms this age-old practice: "Repent *and be baptized every one of you* . . . . The promise is for you *and your children* and for all who are far off—for all whom the Lord our God will call" (Acts 2:38–39).

Jesus received little children as kingdom citizens. Most nations require a probation period, a proficiency test, and a sworn oath of immigrants who wish to become citizens. But without imposing any obligations they grant citizenship to children born on their soil. Jesus appears to concur with that practice: "Let the little children come to me, and do not hinder them, for the kingdom of heaven belongs to such as these" (Matt. 19:14). The state issues a birth certificate as proof of citizenship. God gives such recognition to children of believers by the sacrament of baptism.

The covenantal line through families continues in the New Testament. More than once we read in the New Testament that the apostles baptized whole households when they came to faith. Paul assures the Philippian jailer: "Believe in the Lord Jesus, and you will be saved—you and your household" (Acts 16:31). When they heard the gospel, "he and all his family were baptized" (Acts 16:33).

God's promise precedes our response. God initiates the covenant bond with his promises. He requires no thought-out response before he calls us by baptism into covenant fellowship.

When covenant children reach the age of discretion, they have to answer God's claim with a yes or a no. They need the regenerating power of God's Spirit to make the right choice. If they obey, God will grant them his covenant blessings. If they disobey, they bring on themselves the covenant curses. Their baptism reminds them that they cannot avoid that choice.

The Church Says

Should infants, too, be baptized?

Yes.
Infants as well as adults
    are in God's covenant and are his people.
They, no less than adults, are promised
    the forgiveness of sin through Christ's blood
    and the Holy Spirit who produces faith.

Therefore, by baptism, the mark of the covenant,
    infants should be received into the Christian church
    and should be distinguished from the children
        of unbelievers.
This was done in the Old Testament by circumcision,
    which was replaced in the New Testament by baptism.
(Heidelberg Catechism Q. & A. 74)

Hotseat Question

Do you regret (not) having been baptized at this point in your life?

Check It Out

Genesis 17:1–14; Matthew 19:13–14; Acts 2:38–39, 10:47, 16:31; 1 Corinthians 7:14; Colossians 2:8–15

| QUEST **38** | Why do you belong at the Lord's table? | *After we make public profession of faith, God's people not only invite us, but also expect us to join them in celebrating the Lord's Supper. But what right do we have to participate? This question asks us to look into our motives for sharing in this sacrament. What draws us?* |

Some Possible Answers

Because I belong to Christ. By giving us faith, God's Spirit has grafted us into Jesus, the living vine. Because we belong to him, our Host invites us to feast on the living Bread: "Take and eat; this is my body" (Matt. 26:26). We belong at the table because we draw our very lives from the One who calls us there.

Because I belong to his body. By joining other believers around the Lord's table we celebrate most deeply our common bond in Christ. Paul writes, "Because there is one loaf, we, who are many, are one body, for we all partake of the one loaf" (1 Cor. 10:17). Our absence from the table leaves a gap in the (comm)union of saints. Like all sisters and brothers, we belong at this vital family dinner.

Because I need his grace. We belong at the table even though we don't deserve to be there. By our participation we confess that we are sinners whose eternal life depends on Christ's sacrifice symbolized by this meal. Precisely because we know we're unworthy, we reach out for God. Otherwise we would turn up our noses at this feast that he lays out for beggars of his grace.

Because I still need to grow in faith. Sure, we know what Christ did for us. The Lord's Supper tells us nothing new. But we have not yet arrived. Our faith needs to grow beyond sound doctrine. We need to experience, to celebrate more deeply, what we know.

We belong at the Lord's table because we need to see and to touch and to feel what he has done for us. By his Spirit Jesus fleshes out our head knowledge into full participation in his body and blood.

Because I should show what he has done for me. What Jesus did for us we may never keep to ourselves. We need to share it. His call to fulfill the Great Commission spans every segment of our lives. But it begins here, at his table. Here we publicly declare to all who will look and listen that the living Bread who comes from heaven offers eternal life to all who will feed on him. Paul writes, "For whenever you eat this bread and drink this cup, you proclaim the Lord's death until he comes" (1 Cor. 11:26).

The Church Says

**Who are to come
to the Lord's table?**

Those who are displeased with themselves
    because of their sins,
but who nevertheless trust
    that their sins are pardoned
    and that their continuing weakness is covered
      by the suffering and death of Christ,
and who also desire more and more
    to strengthen their faith
    and to lead a better life.

Hypocrites and those who are unrepentant, however,
eat and drink judgment on themselves.

(Heidelberg Catechism Q. & A. 81)

Hotseat Question

Does anything in your life hamper your participation in the Lord's Supper?

Check It Out

Matthew 11:28–30; 1 Corinthians 11:17–34

<table>
<tr><td>

QUEST
39

</td><td>

What does participation in the Lord's Supper mean to you?

</td><td>

Participation in communion means nothing in and of itself. Unless we know what the Lord's Supper symbolizes, it will not help us grow in faith. It will just gobble up precious worship time. Only if we understand what we're doing will God's Spirit use this sacrament's riches of talking, touching, and tasting to nourish our souls on Christ.

</td></tr>
</table>

Some Possible Answers

That Jesus sacrificed his body and blood for me. Bread and wine do not physically turn into the body and blood of the Lord. But by their use Jesus, through his Spirit, feeds us on his grace. He demonstrates the life-giving effect his sacrifice on Calvary has on us. That's why Jesus tells us: "Take and eat; this is my body. . . . Drink from it, all of you. This is my blood of the covenant, which is poured out for many for the forgiveness of sins" (Matt. 26:26–28).

That I fully depend on Christ for my eternal life. As we continuously depend on food to sustain our physical life, so we need constant fellowship with Jesus to stay alive spiritually. By eating the bread and drinking the wine at the Lord's table we confess that we have no other source of eternal life. We find it only in the risen Lord who by his sacrifice triumphed over death. Jesus promises, "Whoever eats my flesh and drinks my blood has eternal life, and I will raise him up at the last day. For my flesh is real food and my blood is real drink" (John 6:54–55).

It means that I celebrate my unity with Christ. The Lord's Supper is not a funeral service but a celebration. It dwells not on the gory details of Jesus' sacrifice but on its hard-won effects. By the gift of his Spirit Jesus ties our hearts ever more closely to himself. Jesus promised: "I will not leave you as orphans; I will come to you. Before long, the world will not see me anymore, but you will see me. Because I live, you also will live. On that day you will realize that I am in my Father, and you are in me, and I am in you" (John 14:18–20).

It means that I celebrate my unity with my brothers and sisters in Christ. We come to the table of the Lord not as individuals but as family members. We communally share this meal according to Christ's command. That is why we need to iron out our difficulties with one another *before* we celebrate the sacrament. No discord may break the blessed bond of fellowship we enjoy in him. For this same reason we ought not to celebrate communion in small groups or congregational fragments. We celebrate as a community where all are invited and all are welcome.

The Church Says

It means
to accept with a believing heart
the entire suffering and death of Christ
and by believing
to receive forgiveness of sins and eternal life.

But it means more.
Through the Holy Spirit, who lives both in Christ and in us,
we are united more and more to Christ's blessed body.
And so, although he is in heaven and we are on earth,
we are flesh of his flesh and bone of his bone.
And we forever live on and are governed by one Spirit,
as members of our body are by one soul.

(*Heidelberg Catechism* A. 76)

Hotseat Question

What should you feel as you participate at the Lord's table?

Check It Out

Matthew 26:26–29; John 6:35–58

QUEST
40

What do you expect communion to do for you?

Some people come to the Lord's table with overblown expectations. They feel really let down when the Monday morning blues hit them as forcefully as ever. Others have such low expectations that they impatiently tolerate this sacrament as just another religious chore. If we want to avoid disappointment and still allow ourselves to enjoy the fruits of this God-given privilege, it's important that we be realistic about the sacrament.

Some Possible Answers

It helps me grow in faith. The Lord's Supper helps us experience the full reality of what Jesus does for us. By engaging our senses, it reinforces the written and spoken Word.

Through the supper the Holy Spirit nurtures our faith to make it grow. He gives us a clearer understanding of the central truth of the gospel. He also assures us that Jesus offers his salvation to us personally.

It strengthens my bond to Christ. Because Jesus himself is present with us at the supper through his Spirit, he draws us closer to himself. Our love for him increases as we experience his gift of grace to us. Monday mornings may be just as difficult as before. But our bond to Jesus will help us face the new week with renewed commitment to meet its God-given challenges.

It strengthens our bond to fellow believers. As we experience in the sacrament how deeply Jesus loves us, we also grow in our love for each other—even when differences among us threaten to turn into full-blown divisions. By celebrating communion together, we remind ourselves and each other of how much we have in common. We share one Lord, one Spirit, and one salvation. Whatever separates us shrinks back into proper perspective as we share the body and blood of the Lord. Our disagreements will not magically dissolve. But through this communal meal, we learn to tolerate our differences and to put them to their God-intended, good use.

It will motivate me to serve God better. The Lord's Supper is a covenant meal. When we share it together with our risen Lord, we realize that he calls us to fulfill our part as he fulfills his. He gave his life for us. He expects us to give our lives to him. By sharing bread and wine, we confess that we are under obligation to him. No longer may we follow our own sinful, human desires.

We must now follow the Spirit of Christ. We must walk as Jesus walked and sacrifice as he did. "Anyone who does not take his cross and follow me is not worthy of me. Whoever finds his life will lose it, and whoever loses his life for my sake will find it" (Matt. 10:38–39).

The Church Says

This banquet is a spiritual table
at which Christ communicates himself to us
with all his benefits.
At that table he makes us enjoy himself
as much as the merits of his suffering and death,
as he nourishes, strengthens, and comforts
our poor, desolate souls
   by the eating of his flesh,
and relieves and renews them
   by the drinking of his blood.

In short,
by the use of this holy sacrament
we are moved to a fervent love
of God and our neighbors.

(Belgic Confession Article 35)

Hotseat Question

Do you feel your congregation celebrates communion often enough? Why or why not?

Check It Out

1 John 3:11–24

Earth's Heavenly Body

(Quests 41–50)

QUEST 41 What is this church to which Jesus calls you?

By making public profession of faith we commit our lives to Christ and promise to be living members of his church. In order to understand how we fit into that body, we should know what it is and how it lives in the world.

Some Possible Answers

The church is the people of God. In its widest sense, "church" refers to all believers everywhere, throughout the ages—all of those whom Jesus calls to be his chosen people who will live with him forever in the New Jerusalem. In their rich diversity believers find unity in their faith and commitment to him.

Although we can only see fragments of this body at any one time or place in this world, we know that our Lord will make our oneness forever visible in the next.

The church is the worshiping community. Since it is impossible for *all* believers to regularly get together, the body of Christ is subdivided into small cells called congregations. Bound by worship, fellowship, and mutual service, these congregations make the body of Christ visible in a given time and place.

The Bible commands us to show our membership in the universal church by faithfully joining with our fellow believers in the local church: "Let us not give up meeting together, as some are in the habit of doing, but let us encourage one another—and all the more as you see the Day approaching" (Heb. 10:25).

The Church is the Christ-confessing community. Our shared confession that Jesus is Savior and Lord binds all believers together. However, this does not mean that we agree on all matters of faith. We have confessional differences that split us into denominations.

If we think of congregations as cells of the body, we might think of denominations as larger structures, such as organs or bones. Confessional differences may never set Christians against each other. We must continue to work together. And yet the Spirit allows each denomination to make its own unique contribution to the church as a whole.

Still, we look forward to the day when God will dissolve our doctrinal differences by perfecting our understanding.

The church is God's serving community. When they leave church buildings, believers remain church members. Everything they do, they do as representatives of their Lord.

Church membership involves all of life. Believers continue to serve each other during the week. And as representatives of Christ's church, they serve his world: on the job, in the marketplace, and on the beach. Jesus has entrusted them with the task of bringing the good news in word and deed. Through that service he continues to add others to his body until the day he returns.

The Church Says

> **What do you believe**
> **concerning the "holy catholic church"?**
>
> I believe that the Son of God,
>   through his Spirit and Word,
>   out of the entire human race,
>   from the beginning of the world to its end,
> gathers, protects, and preserves for himself
>   a community chosen for eternal life
>   and united in true faith.
> And of this community I am and always will be
>   a living member.
>
> *(Heidelberg Catechism Q. & A. 54)*

Hotseat Question

Do you really feel like you belong? Why or why not?

Check It Out

Ephesians 2:11–22; 1 Peter 2:4–12; Revelation 5:9–10

<table>
<tr><td>

QUEST

42

</td><td>

What's your favorite biblical image of the church?

</td><td>

The proverb still rings true: a picture is worth a thousand words. The Bible presents us with many word-pictures to help us understand this mysterious church to which it calls us. Can you list some?

</td></tr>
</table>

Some Possible Answers

The body of Christ. "The body is a unit, though it is made up of many parts; and though all its parts are many, they form one body. So it is with Christ . . . . You are the body of Christ, and each one of you is a part of it" (1 Cor. 12:12,27).

The people of God. "But you are a chosen people, a royal priesthood, a holy nation, a people belonging to God, that you may declare the praises of him who called you out of darkness into his wonderful light. Once you were not a people, but now you are the people of God" (1 Peter 2:9–10).

The bride of Christ. "Husbands, love your wives, just as Christ loved the church and gave himself up for her to make her holy, cleansing her by the washing with water through the word, and to present her to himself as a radiant church, without stain or wrinkle or any other blemish, but holy and blameless" (Eph. 5:25–27).

Branches of the vine. "I am the vine; you are the branches. If a man remains in me and I in him, he will bear much fruit" (John 15:5).

Salt of the earth. "You are the salt of the earth. But if the salt loses its saltiness, how can it be made salty again? It is no longer good for anything, except to be thrown out and trampled by men" (Matt. 5:13).

Light of the world. "You are the light of the world. A city on a hill cannot be hidden. Neither do people light a lamp and put it under a bowl. . . . Let your light shine before men, that they may see your good deeds and praise your Father in heaven" (Matt. 5:14–16).

God's building. Don't you know that you yourselves are God's temple and that God's Spirit lives in you? . . . God's temple is sacred, and you are that temple" (1 Cor. 3:16–17).

Exiles. "Dear friends, I urge you, as aliens and strangers in the world, to abstain from sinful desires, which war against your soul" (1 Pet. 2:11–12).

The new creation. "Therefore, if anyone is in Christ, he is a new creation; the old has gone, the new has come!" (2 Cor. 5:17).

The family of God. "Yet to all who received him, to those who believed in his name, he gave the right to become children of God—children born not of natural descent, nor of human decision or a husband's will, but born of God" (John 1:12–13).

The Church Says

> We believe and confess
> one single catholic or universal church—
> a holy congregation and gathering
> of true Christian believers,
> awaiting their entire salvation in Jesus Christ
> being washed by his blood.
> and sanctified and sealed by the Holy Spirit.
>
> (*Belgic Confession Article 27*)

Hotseat Question

Does your church live up to this image?

Check It Out

Romans 11:11–24; 1 Corinthians 12:12–31

<table>
<tr><td>

QUEST

43

</td><td>

How do you know that your congregation is a true church of Christ?

</td><td>

With a bewildering number to choose from, how do we tell a true church from a false one? How do we know if by joining a particular fellowship we worship God or Satan? Many differences between churches run only skin deep. But what about the wolves in sheep's clothing who lie through their teeth when they claim to be the church of Christ? They're out there too. And what about the many well-meaning churches that have slowly drifted away from the truth, wandering out onto the slippery slope that descends into hell? How can we be sure that our church isn't one of them?

</td></tr>
</table>

Some Possible Answers

My church faithfully proclaims the gospel of Christ. All churches have their blemishes, warts, and annoying quirks. But what clearly distinguishes a true church from a false church is its answer to the question Jesus asked of Peter: "Who do you say I am?" (Matt. 16:15). This confession lies at the core of the true church's preaching, teaching, and ministry. Without it our church is a dying hulk with its heart torn out. With it, we rest secure on the bedrock of this confessing disciple: "I tell you that you are Peter, and on this rock I will build my church, and the gates of Hades will not overcome it" (Matt. 16:18).

Sermons may be boring, singing uninspiring, members undependable. Even churches with such handicaps can be living members of Christ's body. The key is in the message: if your church faithfully proclaims God's Word, you belong there.

My church obediently administers the sacraments. In response to the direct commands of our Lord the true church baptizes its members and celebrates communion, using the actions and words that Jesus taught. Through the sacraments the church speaks volumes about God's great love for us and provides the channel by which the Spirit of Jesus feeds us on his grace.

It practices church discipline. In obedience to God's Word the true church dares to discipline. Members discipline themselves. In all humility and love they also discipline each other. They encourage and admonish one another as circumstances require.

When mutual discipline fails, the leaders of the church do their part to break sin's enslaving grip and maintain the holiness of the fellowship. Jesus himself places this awesome responsibility on the church: "I tell you the truth, whatever you bind on earth will be bound in heaven, and whatever you loose on earth will be loosed in heaven" (Matt. 18:18).

The Church Says

The true church can be recognized
if it has the following marks:
    The church engages in the pure preaching
      of the gospel;
    it makes use of the pure administration of the sacraments
      as Christ instituted them;
    it practices church discipline
      for correcting faults.
In short, it governs itself
according to the pure Word of God.

(Belgic Confession Article 29)

Hotseat Question

If you think your church is straying from the truth, what should you do?

Check It Out

Matthew 16:13–20; 1 Corinthians 11:27–34; Galatians 5:1–5; Revelation 3:7–13

QUEST **44**	**How should you, as a member of Christ's church, be separate from the world?**

Members of Christ's church are holy. That doesn't mean they are perfect (yet). It means that Christ, through the gospel, separates them from the rest of rebellious humanity and makes them people dedicated to the service of God. In what ways should we, as members of that holy church, be separate from the world? How should we dare to be different—to be in the world but not of it?

Some Possible Answers

My values are different. The things God's people consider important contrast sharply with the values of the world. For us pleasing God, not ourselves or others, is the highest virtue. We deem raising covenant children in God's ways a higher achievement than reaching the top rungs of the corporate ladder. We consider teen virginity a plus not a minus. We'd rather pay Christian school tuition than use the money for airfare to Hawaii. Our heroes are servants, not big shots. We care more what the inside looks like than the outside.

What the world values, we disdain. What we consider crucial, it ignores.

My goals are different. Jesus tells us, "Do not worry about your life, what you will eat or drink; or about your body, what you will wear. Is not life more important than food, and the body more important than clothes? . . . But seek first [your heavenly Father's] kingdom and his righteousness, and all these things will be given to you as well" (Matt. 6:25,33). Our goal is God's kingdom, not our own; to contribute, not to consume; to strive for the life to come, not just to make the best of this one.

My way of doing things is different. God calls us to obey, to do things his way. Therefore, we may not be pragmatists. Our first question may not be "Will it work?" but "Is this God's will for me?" King Saul found out the hard way that "To obey is better than sacrifice, and to heed is better than the fat of rams" (1 Sam. 15:22).

Walking the world's crooked roads will never put us back onto God's path. Those ways never intersect.

My standards are different. Tastes vary. Fashions change. But the Bible's standards for our life don't. That may put us out of step with the world. Gaudy, revealing, expensive clothes may be "in." But with God they're always out. Paul says: ". . . dress modestly, with decency and propriety, not with braided hair or gold or pearls or expensive clothes, but with good deeds" (1 Tim. 2:910).

We need not walk around in eighteenth-century garb. But our clothes, homes, vehicles, and life-styles should reflect God's standards. Sometimes we must stick out like a sore thumb—for Jesus' sake.

The Church Says

> To preserve this unity more effectively,
> it is the duty of all believers,
>   according to God's Word,
> to separate themselves
> from those who do not belong to the church,
>   in order to join his assembly
>   wherever God has established it,
>   even if civil authorities and royal decrees forbid
>   and death and physical punishment result.
>
> *(Belgic Confession Article 28)*

Hotseat Question

Where do you find it most difficult to stay separate from the world?

Check It Out

Genesis 12; 2 Corinthians 6:14–7:1; 1 John 2:15–17

| QUEST 45 | What task has the Lord given us to do as a church? |

Church membership has little to do with having our names on some official church register. Although record keeping has its place, it cannot and does not replace what real membership is all about. Being members in Jesus' church means that we actively participate in the body. It means that we don't just pop by now and then but that we consistently join God's people in doing the work Jesus himself has given us to do. To do our part as living members, we need to know what that common task is.

Some Possible Answers

Grow up. Like any living body, the church must keep growing or it will die. It must continually feed on God's Word. It must learn. It must flex its spiritual muscles in worship and service to prevent them from becoming as limp and useless as those of a bed-ridden patient.

If we exercise the rich gifts Jesus gives us, our fellowship will grow in quality as well as quantity. Paul writes: "Speaking the truth in love, we will in all things grow up into him who is the Head, that is, Christ. From him the whole body, joined and held together by every supporting ligament, grows and builds itself up in love, as each part does its work" (Eph. 4:15–16).

Evangelize. Our Good Shepherd will not rest until he has found all his wandering sheep. We may not either. He invites us to share in that challenging, delightful task of bringing lost sheep back to God. We gather them from far and wide by sharing with them the good news of Jesus and his love. Our Lord commands: "Go and make disciples of all nations, baptizing them in the name of the Father and of the Son and of the Holy Spirit, and teaching them to obey everything I have commanded you" (Matt. 28:19–20).

Care for the poor and oppressed. Jesus not only told people the good news— he also showed it to them. He healed the sick and fed the hungry.

We should too. As his hands in the world, church members not only tell of Jesus' love but also reach out and show it. This deaconal task extends to all believers. Jesus calls us to be generous to the needy within and outside of the household of faith.

Extend Christ's kingdom in the world. As God's army, the church works to reclaim the fallen creation in his name. The marketplace, the theater, and the lab are his. We must bring all areas of life into obedience to our ascended king.

We confess that we will not complete the work of reclaiming creation. Jesus will do so when he returns. But in the meantime we can help his kingdom grow.

The Church Says

Following the apostles, the church is sent—
sent with the gospel of the kingdom
to make disciples of all nations,
to feed the hungry,
and to proclaim the assurance that in the name of
Christ
there is forgiveness of sin and new life
for all who repent and believe—
to tell the news that our world belongs to God.

(Our World Belongs to God, 44)

Hotseat Question

Where can you best help in this great task?

Check It Out

Matthew 28:16–20; Acts 1:1–9; Ephesians 4:1–16

QUEST	What	*When we make public profession of*
46	responsibili-	*faith, we promise to do our fair share in*

<table>
<tr><td>QUEST
46</td><td>What responsibili-ties do you take on as a confessing member?</td><td>*When we make public profession of faith, we promise to do our fair share in the church. Christ asks us to serve the body as the body serves us. Some duties are unique to a few members. Others are shared by all. Can you list some of the tasks you share with all your fellow believers?*</td></tr>
</table>

Some Possible Answers

I promise to participate faithfully in worship. Worship is work. It is central to the task of the church. Our praises, prayers, songs, and offerings weave a rich tapestry to God's glory. By offering to him our very best, we fulfill a central purpose for which he created us. By carefully paying attention to his Word and sharing in the sacraments, we grow in unity with each other and with his will.

God craves this intimate dialogue with his family. So should we.

I promise to study the Word with others. Public profession does not mark our graduation from church school. Our faith-knowledge needs to keep growing as long as we live. And just as others have shared their insights with us, so we should share what we know with others. That way we hand God's covenant truth down through the generations. Whether we participate in church school, societies, clubs, or fellowship groups, we commit ourselves to a life of learning together.

I promise to witness. Not everyone possesses the gifts needed to knock on doors and present the gospel to those who answer. Evangelism takes special skills. But we can all learn to witness where we are.

Talking about the hope that lies within us may not come easily. But with a bit of effort we can learn to be much more open about our faith. God placed us in this dark world to help others see the light.

I promise to contribute my fair share financially. We tend to view our financial contributions to the church as just an administrative detail. But Jesus regards our gifts as a deeply spiritual concern: "For where your treasure is, there your heart will be also" (Matt. 6:21).

As God pours out his riches on us, we must also be rich toward him. "God loves a cheerful giver" (2 Cor. 9:7). Two very accurate measures of our spirituality are what we give and why.

I promise to care for my fellow members. When one part of our body hurts, the whole body hurts. That's why our hands reach out so quickly to free a pinched toe.

In the same way, we cannot let others within the community of saints suffer alone. If our hearts reach out to them, our hands can't be far behind. We serve each other as Christ serves us: sharing, healing, and correcting. When fellow travelers stumble or stray, we humbly and lovingly lend them a hand—Christ's hand.

The Church Says

But all people are obliged
to join and unite with [the church],
keeping the unity of the church
   by submitting to its instruction and discipline,
   by bending their necks under the yoke of Jesus Christ,
   and by serving to build up one another,
according to the gifts God has given them
as members of each other
in the same body.

                                                   (*Belgic Confession Article 28*)

Hotseat Question

Which responsibilities do you find the hardest to fulfill? Why?

Check It Out

2 Corinthians 8:1–12; Ephesians 6:10–18; Hebrews 10:19–25; 1 Peter 3:15

QUEST
47

What gift(s) has Christ given you to share with his church?

Along with tasks we all can do, the church needs services that require specific, unique gifts. Jesus, through his Spirit, distributes such gifts among the members of the body. He calls each one of us to use our gifts for the good of all. What gifts has Christ given you that you can use for our common good?

Some Possible Answers

Prophecy—the ability to publicly proclaim and apply God's Word to the congregation.

Evangelism—the ability to present the gospel clearly and powerfully to those who do not know it.

Teaching—the ability to increase and deepen the faith-knowledge of others.

Faith—the ability to keep the body strongly rooted in Christ, especially in times of crisis or confusion.

Shepherding—the ability to nurture and guide other members.

Music—the ability to accompany or lead congregational singing, join in a vocal group, direct a choir, and so forth.

Financial giving—the ability to provide generously for the financial needs of the community and individual members.

Administration—the ability to manage the business affairs of the church or to provide clerical assistance.

Healing—the ability to bring wholeness to those who suffer physical illness, emotional trauma, or broken relationships.

Leadership—the ability to enable and organize the body to fulfill its responsibilities and goals.

Hospitality—the ability to host and provide fellowship for members and guests alike.

Service—the ability to spend time at helping to do what needs to be done. The church needs willing, efficient, able "gophers."

Counseling—the ability to empathize and to guide hurting people toward wholeness.

Prayer—the ability to intercede for others before God's throne.

Art—the ability to provide creative visuals, liturgies, and poetic responses.

Discernment—the ability to test the spirits and determine whether they are of God.

Encouragement—the gift of stimulating others to fulfill their tasks.

Knowledge—the ability to research and provide helpful information where it is needed.

The Church Says

**What do you understand by
"the communion of saints"?**

First, that believers one and all,
as members of this community,
share in Christ
and in all his treasures and gifts.

Second, that each member
should consider it a duty
to use these gifts
   readily and cheerfully
    for the service and enrichment
     of the other members.

(Heidelberg Catechism Q. & A. 55)

Hotseat Question

How will you find a way to use your gift(s) in the church? Will you wait to be asked?

Check It Out

Romans 12:1–13; 1 Corinthians 12:1–11; Ephesians 4:1–13

As a confessing member you may be called to serve as an officebearer in the church. What are these offices?

All Christians share in the general office of believer. Christ himself has set us apart and calls us to serve him and his kingdom. But the Lord has also provided us with more specific offices that help us fulfill our communal task. Through these offices Jesus himself governs his church. Can you identify these special offices as they function within the Reformed tradition? Within your denomination?

Some Possible Answers

Servant of the Word. Ministers feed the flock of Christ on God's Word. Jesus calls them to preach his Word, teach it, and apply it to the daily lives of his people. He calls them to serve believers by equipping them to be better servants of Christ.

A minister's responsibilities include the following:
1. preaching the Word
2. administering the sacraments
3. conducting the worship service
4. engaging in evangelism and training others in that task
5. engaging in the service of prayer
6. joining with elders and deacons in providing leadership to the flock
7. joining with elders to guide, counsel, and discipline God's people

Elder. In obedience to the requirement of Scripture, we set apart elders to govern us in Christ's name. They provide spiritual supervision over the body and its members.

Elders are called to the following tasks:
1. faithfully providing and supervising worship services
2. providing and supervising regular celebration of the sacraments
3. providing Bible-based guidance and counsel to the members
4. exercising Christian discipline
5. stimulating Christian fellowship and mutual service
6. leading and equipping members in sharing the Word with others

Deacon. Deacons lead the congregation in showing Christ's mercy within and beyond the community of faith. They equip us to be good stewards of the riches with which he entrusts us. Their tasks include the following:

1. assessing needs
2. finding from among us the resources to fill these needs
3. meeting physical needs
4. meeting the accompanying spiritual needs with encouraging words from Scripture
5. relieving those oppressed by injustice
6. training members in stewardly use of their possessions
7. gathering in and disbursing offerings

Others. Some Reformed denominations recognize other particular offices as well. For example, some see the task of an evangelist or a seminary professor as unique enough to warrant distinct offices. Scripture leaves plenty of room for churches to structure their leadership to best fit their situation and needs.

The Church Says

We believe that this true church
ought to be governed according to the spiritual order
that our Lord has taught us in his Word.
   There should be ministers or pastors
      to preach the Word of God
and administer the sacraments.
   There should also be elders and deacons,
      along with the pastors,
to make up the council of the church.

(Belgic Confession Article 30)

Hotseat Question

How can you help officebearers fulfill their tasks well?

Check It Out

Acts 6:1–6; Acts 20:27–31; Ephesians 4:11–13; 1 Timothy 3:1–13; 2 Timothy 4:1–5

| QUEST 49 | If you want to see something change in the church, whom do you approach? | *Reformed churches keep reforming themselves. They do not change just for the sake of change. They change to make themselves more obedient to God's Word and better equipped to bring the gospel to each new age. But even good changes that were not dealt with or implemented in an orderly way have torn churches apart. If you want to see something taught or done differently in your church, to whom should you take it? Who has the proper authority to evaluate and carry out your suggestion?* |

Some Possible Answers

Present it to my church. Christ rules the church through his Word. He entrusts the task of keeping his body faithful to that Word to the duly-appointed officebearers. Therefore, authority for regulating and running the church rests with the council made up of the pastor(s), elders, and deacons.

If the change you seek is a local matter, affecting only your congregation, this is the body you should address. You can write a letter or attend a council meeting in person. After members of the council have discussed your suggestion, they should notify you of their response.

Present it to classis. The scope of your idea may extend to other regional churches of your denomination. If so, your proposal should go to classis.

Classis consists of delegates from local church councils. It meets two or three times yearly to take up matters of common concern and to tackle projects too large for individual congregations to handle.

To get your idea on the floor of classis you should first submit it to your local council. If council agrees, their representatives will take the matter to classis on your behalf. If council disagrees, it will advise you how you may bring the matter to the wider assemblies yourself.

Present it to synod. If your idea affects your whole denomination, it should go to synod. Synod is the widest assembly of the church, made up of delegates from each classis. It meets annually or biannually to address matters affecting all churches within the denomination. Synod carries ultimate responsibility for denominational structures, ministries, and confessional standards.

You place your idea before synod by asking your council to endorse your suggestion. Your council asks classis to do the same and take it to synod. If classis balks at the proposal, your council may take it to synod itself.

The Church Says

We also believe that
although it is useful and good
for those who govern the churches
to establish and set up
a certain order among themselves
for maintaining the bond of the church,
they ought always to guard against deviating
from what Christ,
our only Master,
has ordained
for us.
So we accept only what is proper
to maintain harmony and unity
and to keep all in obedience
to God.

(Belgic Confession Article 32)

Hotseat Question

What changes would you like to see in your church? Why?

Check It Out

Acts 15:1–35

QUEST **50**	As a church member how can you stay on the "straight and narrow"?

By making public profession we commit ourselves to following Jesus. But he leads us on a challenging road. Sometimes we will stray from it. We may knuckle under to temptation. Or Satan may blind-side us, fooling us into thinking that good is bad and bad is good. Or we may lose our way in the murky gray areas of life. How can we follow the light of God's Word back to the true Way?

Some Possible Answers

By self-discipline. Our responsibility to obey God in all we do remains first and foremost our own. We're personally accountable to him for our thoughts, words, and deeds.

If we fall into sin, we need to repent. We need to confess our sin and get on with God's work, ditching the works of darkness. If others fail to come to our rescue, we may not use that as an excuse to wallow in our disobedience. God makes his covenant with each one of us personally. Our baptism testifies to that.

By mutual discipline. Jesus commands, "If your brother sins against you, go and show him his fault, just between the two of you. If he listens to you, you have won your brother over" (Matt. 18:15). God asks that we look out for each other, correcting each other humbly and lovingly. That takes courage. But we may not let others commit spiritual suicide without clearly warning and helping them.

Jesus continues, "But if he will not listen, take one or two others along, so that 'every matter may be established by the testimony of two or three witnesses'" (Matt. 18:16). Most of us respond best to this informal, mutual form of Christian discipline. Through it our Good Shepherd guides his sheep by letting them shepherd each other.

By official church discipline. Jesus continues, "If he refuses to listen to them, tell it to the church; and if he refuses to listen even to the church, treat him as you would a pagan or a tax collector. I tell you the truth, whatever you bind on earth will be bound in heaven, and whatever you loose on earth will be loosed in heaven" (Matt. 18:17–18).

If members refuse to heed other members, consistory will seek to bring such people back to obedience by prayer and repeated visits. While encouraging full participation in all church activities, council may prohibit such wandering sheep from participating in the sacraments. These it restricts to believers who show their faith through their godly walk.

If council's repeated efforts to reach unfaithful members fail, council must excommunicate these wayward brothers and sisters from the church. No longer members, they become the objects of evangelism—as are all others who live in the darkness of unbelief.

The Church Says

Those who, though called Christians,
    profess unchristian teachings or live unchristian lives,
and after repeated and loving counsel,
    refuse to abandon their errors and wickedness,
and after being reported to the church, that is, to its officers,
    fail to respond also to their admonition—
such persons the officers exclude
        from the Christian fellowship
    by withholding the sacraments from them,
and God himself excludes them from the kingdom of Christ.

Such persons,
    when promising and demonstrating genuine reform,
are received again
    as members of Christ
    and of his church.

(Heidelberg Catechism Answer 85)

Hotseat Question

How can you become more disciplined in your walk with God?

Check It Out

Matthew 18:10–20; 1 Corinthians 5:1–6:11; Galatians 6:1–5

Seven Son-Days a Week

(Quests 51–60)

| QUEST **51** | What word best describes the life-style you should adopt as a Christian? | *A serf living in medieval Europe had exactly one life-style to choose from: poverty-stricken farm slave. If he objected, he was quickly relieved of his head. Today the freedom and prosperity many of us enjoy face us with a crucial choice: how shall we live? With so many options, what life-style should we pursue: punker, peace activist, patriot, capitalist, conservationist, consumer, liberal, couch potato?* |

Some Possible Answers

Steward. God puts us on spaceship earth to work, not to waste our time and his gifts. He grants us control over creation so that we can develop and unfold its riches for his glory. He promises us that responsible effort will meet with his rich blessing. He provides generously so that we may also take time to celebrate and rejoice.

We may idolize neither our work nor our recreational time. His love frees us from slavery to work or play.

Servant. Our foot-washing Lord shows us how to live: "Whoever wants to be great among you must be your servant, and whoever wants to be first must be slave of all" (Mark 10:43–44). Our Christ-mindedness rescues us from selfishness. Far from turning us into throw rugs for others to walk over, it enables us to serve our neighbors as Jesus would: giving them what they really need rather than what they want.

Ambassador. In Luke 7:28 Jesus tells us, "Among those born of women there is no one greater than John; yet the one who is least in the kingdom of God is greater then he."

The reason for Jesus' statement is simple: any child of God today has a message much richer than the messages of all the prophets before him. John could only say Messiah was on his way. We can tell the world "Messiah has come!"

Child. Jesus teaches, "Unless you change and become like little children, you will never enter the kingdom of heaven" (Matt. 18:3–4). Jesus expects us to humble ourselves, to recognize our total dependence on him. If we make ourselves small in our own eyes, we will be great in our heavenly Father's eyes: "See that you do not look down on one of these little ones. For I tell you that their angels in heaven always see the face of my Father in heaven" (Matt. 18:10).

Temple. The Bible commands us to live moral, clean lives. Paul writes, "Flee from sexual immorality. All other sins a man commits are outside his body, but he who sins sexually sins against his own body. Do you not know that your body is a temple of the Holy Spirit, who is in you, whom you have received from God?" (1 Cor. 6:18–19).

The Church Says

> . . . that I give up anything
> rather than go against [God's] will in any way.
>
> (*Heidelberg Catechism A. 94*)

> We should . . . thoroughly detest [unchastity]
> and, married or single,
> live decent and chaste lives.
>
> (*Heidelberg Catechism A. 108*)

> [God] forbids all greed
> and pointless squandering of his gifts.
>
> (*Heidelberg Catechism A. 110*)

> That I do whatever I can
>   for my neighbor's good,
> that I treat others
>   as I would like them to treat me,
> and that I work faithfully
>   so that I may share with those in need.
>
> (*Heidelberg Catechism A. 111*)

Hotseat Question

How consistently do you live a Christian life?

Check It Out

Exodus 20:1–17; Ephesians 5:1–6:9

QUEST **52**	Do you find "every day with Jesus sweeter than the day before"?

Using the language of an old gospel-meeting rouser, this question asks us to monitor our daily walk with our Lord. How are we doing? Are we growing in our faith? Are we drawing closer to Christ? Is our relationship to him improving? Or are we standing still—or even sliding backwards? The Bible urges us to stay alert. Most people who fall back into darkness do not make a conscious decision to do so—they just drift away. We musn't let that happen to us!

Some Possible Answers

No, I see growth, but not every day. Our relationship with the Lord has its ups and downs. One day we feel closer to him than the next. The downs are never his fault. He remains faithful. But we do not necessarily have to blame ourselves either. Sometimes we feel distant from God because of the circumstances in which we find ourselves, the stretch of the Way we have to travel. Even the psalmists dared to complain that God seemed far away from them during troubled times.

Yet even through hard times we may experience growth if we do what the psalmists did: cling in faith to our great God. He will come through. Suffering may for a time make God seem far from us. It may rob us of the sweetness of our relationship to Christ. But it cannot stunt our spiritual growth. Only our neglect can do that.

Yes, at least most days. Some of us have the uncanny ability to absorb life's blows and turn their punch into spiritual energy. Like judo experts, we may be able to deflect the force of our opposition, making it help us rather than hurt us. On good days we celebrate. On bad days we learn. Good and bad times, each in their own way, deepen and strengthen our bond to Christ. As M. Scott Peck observed in his book *The Road Less Traveled,* "the only obstacle to our spiritual growth is laziness."

Every day, no; every year or decade, yes. When children consult the growth chart daily, they become easily discouraged. They grow so slowly they cannot measure it. Only when they look back to where they were a year or two ago, do they perk up.

In our spiritual life the same thing is often true. We may notice the odd growth spurt but often see nothing on a day-to-day basis. Yet when we look back to where we were in our relationship to God five years ago, we notice we've come a long way. We know more about God and his ways. We experience more deeply our bond to him. And we know better how we may serve him.

The Church Says

Why does God . . . want [the Ten Commandments] preached so pointedly?

First, so that the longer we live
   the more we may come to know our sinfulness
   and the more eagerly look to Christ
     for forgiveness of sins and righteousness.

Second, so that,
   while praying to God for the grace of the Holy Spirit,
we may never stop striving
   to be renewed more and more after God's image,
until after this life we reach our goal:
   perfection.

(Heidelberg Catechism Q. & A. 115)

Hotseat Question

What kind of "spiritual growth chart" do you have? Do you use it regularly?

Check It Out

Ephesians 3:14–21; 1 Peter 1:22–2:5; 2 Peter 3:17–18

| QUEST 53 | What does God want you to say to him in your prayers? | *The* Heidelberg Catechism *considers prayer the most important part of our response to God. That's understandable. We're his children, and he wants us to talk to him. But what should we say to God? Will he be pleased if all we ever manage to send up is a quick "thanks for the grub" before supper or a wish-list of needed items before retiring? If prayer is "the Christian's vital breath," we may need to make it fresher than we usually do. What does God deserve to hear from you?* |

Some Possible Answers

Adoration. God created us to glorify him, to make his name great in the world. We should praise him by the things we do, the things we tell others, *and* the things we tell him. When the splendor of the starry heavens overwhelms us, we should tell him how we marvel at his majesty. When we delight in scampering sea otters or the brilliant colors of fall, we should compliment him on his handiwork.

We can glorify God anywhere, anytime. We need not assume a classical pose (too risky with a steering wheel in your hands!). More than any master artist, God craves our feedback. And he deserves it.

Confession. When we pray, we should openly recognize who we are. In all humility we should tell God we do not deserve his attention, his love, or his forgiveness. We must ask forgiveness for the things we do that hurt him. Unspoken guilt lingers to hurt both of us. Only when we take the effort to openly confess our sins will we experience the healing of God's forgiving grace.

Thanksgiving. No words in all creation sound as much like music to God's ears as a heartfelt, "Thanks, Dad!" We should discipline ourselves to become more observant of God's blessings. We're experts at remembering what we want. But when God comes through for us, we often either fail to notice or forget to acknowledge his blessings. Our prayer life need not be regimented, but it should be disciplined.

Supplication. We honor God when we ask him for the things we need. Far from discouraging us from doing so, Jesus promises, "Ask and it will be given to you; seek and you will find; knock and the door will be opened to you" (Matt. 7:7). And if God finds it better not to answer us with a yes right away, Jesus encourages us to go right on asking. He concludes the parable of the persistent widow with these words: "Will not God bring about justice for his chosen ones, who cry out to him day and night? Will he keep putting them off? I tell you, he will see that they get justice, and quickly" (Luke 18:7–8).

The Church Says

Why do Christians need to pray?

Because prayer is the most important part
   of the thankfulness God requires of us.
And also because God gives his grace and Holy Spirit
only to those who pray continually and groan inwardly,
    asking God for these gifts
    and thanking him for them.

(*Heidelberg Catechism Q. & A. 116*)

Hotseat Question

Should you pray when you don't feel like it, or is that hypocritical?

Check It Out

Psalm. 50:7–15; Psalm 100; Matthew 6:5–15; 1 Thessalonians 5:16–18

QUEST 54

Why does God sometimes answer no to your prayers?

Many argue that it's always our unbelief that makes God say no. If we only believe "hard" enough, God will give us what we ask. That's small comfort! It leaves us not only feeling the sting of our unfulfilled need but also beginning to doubt the quality of our faith. The real answer lies elsewhere. True children understand that Dad sometimes has to say no. Even Jesus got a firm no in Gethsemane when he begged his Father not to make him drink the bitter cup. But as a true Son he added, "But, Father, your will be done." He knew that Father knows best. Can you give some reasons why God may also have to deny your requests?

Some Possible Answers

Because I haven't asked earnestly. The power of prayer does not lie in the act of praying itself. Prayer isn't magic. It won't let us manipulate God.

The power of prayer lies in God's willingness to listen to his children and to be convinced by them. More than once the Scriptures tell us that God listened to the pleas of one of his children and repented of the evil he was planning to send his disobedient people (Ex. 32:14).

If we pray mechanically, our petitions fall on deaf ears. God seeks real communication, not rote gibberish.

Because his timing is better than mine. Sometimes God plans to come through for us, but he asks us to wait. We only see the present. God in one glimpse sees past and future as well. He asks us to be patient because he knows the best time to fulfill our need. Peter tells us, "With the Lord a day is like a thousand years, and a thousand years are like a day. The Lord is not slow in keeping his promise, as some understand slowness. He is patient with you, not wanting anyone to perish, but everyone to come to repentance" (2 Pet. 3:8–9).

Because what I'm asking may damage me or someone else. What kind of a parent would give Junior a loaded rifle just because he asked for it? God will surely fill our needs. But he will not honor requests that will irreparably injure us or others. We wouldn't want him to! God sees consequences we can't even imagine. True childlike trust asks, but does not demand. It humbly rests in God's infinitely greater wisdom.

Because he has something better in store for me. Often God's "no" really hurts us in the short term. But many years later we discover that he made things turn out better than we ever expected. True prayer remains an ongoing dialogue. His children ask, and God responds. In turn, his children ask again. And God responds again. That ongoing give and take of seeking and searching for God's will is what a real life of prayer is all about.

The Church Says

Your will be done on earth as it is in heaven means

Help us and all people
    to reject our own wills
    and to obey your will without any back talk.
    Your will alone is good.

Help us one and all to carry out the work we are called to,
    as willingly and faithfully as the angels in heaven.
(Heidelberg Catechism A. 124)

Hotseat Question

Do you always need to find out why God says no?

Check It Out

Exodus 32:9–14; Matthew 26:35–46

QUEST
55

Besides prayer, what other ways do you have of daily staying in touch with your Lord?

On the average, American Christians spend more than two hours per day glued to the tube. But we find less than ten minutes a day for our God. That's our loss as well as his. Unless we discipline ourselves to seek him, our spiritual lives remain impoverished shells of what they could be.

How do you stay in touch?

Some Possible Answers

I study Scripture. Nothing replaces personal Bible reading—not sermons, group studies, or even family devotions. God speaks to us in all these ways. But the one-on-one exchange of digging into the Word often meets our personal needs the best. It forms the platform from which we can meaningfully participate in communal learning settings.

I read Christian literature. Consulting the reflections and experiences of others helps us grow in the Lord. Christian literature widens our vision by providing us with fresh ways of seeing God through the eyes of others. But we must constantly check to be sure that what we read reflects scriptural truth. That's why Christian literature can add to, but never replace, our Bible reading.

I enjoy Christian music. Whether we sing like a lark or a rusty door hinge, music provides us with a powerful way of communicating with God. Lyrics and melodies can reach us in ways that other means of communication cannot. If we sing, or sing along, our words surely reach God. If we just listen, our spirits carry the message to heaven all the same.

I take time out to reflect. Many Christians find meditation a powerful way of meeting God. When we clear our schedules and our minds of all the busyness of daily living, we can center our attention on God himself. That takes discipline, because we're so readily distracted. Sometimes a verse from Scripture, a biblical image, or an important personal experience can help us focus on God. When we create space in our minds and hearts, God can fill it with his rest.

I worship God in nature. Tromping through the bush or just jogging Rover through the park can put us in touch with our Creator. When we see and feel his artistry, we see the Artist again. We experience the splendors he has laid out for us. And we give him the glory.

I tune in to Christian broadcasting. God does not ignore the wonders of technology. He's in transmitters and video tubes as well as the rustling grass. Many programs responsibly put us in touch with him over the airwaves. But we need to stay on our guard. By searching Scripture we must ferret out the good from the bad. The great Deceiver also knows transistors from transponders.

The Church Says

> *Hallowed be your name* means,

> Help us to really know you,
> to bless, worship, and praise you
>   for all your works
>   and for all that shines forth from them:
>   your almighty power, wisdom, kindness,
>   justice, mercy, and truth.

> And it means,

> Help us to direct all our living—
>   what we think, say, and do—
> so that your name will never be blasphemed because of us
> but always honored and praised.

(Heidelberg Catechism A. 122)

Hotseat Question

Do you build devotional times into your schedule? How?

Check It Out

Psalm 139; Colossians 3:1–4, 15–17

QUEST 56	You pledge to serve only God. Which idols in your life tempt you to break that promise?

We think of idols as gruesome statues that pagans worshiped long ago. We cannot imagine ourselves actually falling into the same sin as they. But we do it all the time! We constantly invent new idols around which we wrap our hearts and lives. Whenever we enslave ourselves to anything instead of serving God, we've created an idol. We can spot idols by checking whether we sacrifice too many of our energies or resources to any one person or thing. Are we so addicted that we ignore God's command in other areas of life? Where are the idols that bring you to your knees?

Some Possible Answers

Wealth. Greed for material possessions makes us waste too much precious time trying to make money. We ignore more important things. To the almighty buck we sacrifice time to rest and celebrate. We sacrifice time to do our part in church. We sacrifice our marriages, families, and friendships.

In the end this idol leaves us dirt poor—despite a fat bank account. Surrounding ourselves with meaningless junk does not fill the aching void inside. Jesus commands, "I tell you, use worldly wealth to gain friends for yourselves, so that when it is gone, you will be welcomed into eternal dwellings . . . . You cannot serve both God and Money" (Luke 16:9,13).

Popularity. The relentles crush of peer pressure makes us sacrifice our loved ones, our self-respect, and our morality. It slices our God-given unity up into competing, self-centered little cliques. It hollows out our relationships, driving us to use each other for our own ends. Genuine openness goes out the window so that we can maintain our all-important "image."

For a brief moment in the spotlight, we throw away our happiness in this world and the next. For when the spotlight's glare passes from us, this idol leaves us permanently in the dark.

Pleasure. Pleasure is good, not bad. God created us to enjoy life. He promises us eternal life filled with pleasure. But when we make pleasure itself our goal, when we give up everything for the "quick fix," we reduce our lives to the tiresome, always-disappointing search for kicks.

Jesus tells us to forego some pleasures now so that we can do his work. In the long run he will reward us with lasting happiness and joy. "If anyone would come after me, he must deny himself and take up his cross and follow me. For whoever wants to save his life will lose it, but whoever loses his life for me and for the gospel will save it" (Mark 8:34–35).

Fame, alcohol, sex, television, food, cars, parties, laziness, respectability, power, hobbies, pride, and so on.

The Church Says

Idolatry is
   having or inventing something
   in which one trusts in place of or alongside of the only true God,
      who has revealed himself in his Word.

(Heidelberg Catechism A. 95)

Hotseat Question

When you've identified an idol, how do you dismantle it?

Check It Out

1 Corinthians 10:6–14; Galatians 4:8–11; Ephesians 5:5; Philippians 3:17–4:1

QUEST 57

How does God expect you to treat others?

Talk is cheap. And the road to hell is paved with good intentions. God points us to the bottom line: how do we actually treat our neighbors?

Some Possible Answers

The same way I want them to treat me. Jesus commands, "In everything, do to others what you would have them do to you, for this sums up the Law and the Prophets" (Matt. 7:12). This "Golden Rule" sticks us squarely in our neighbor's moccasins. From their perspective we see clearly what God's Word asks of us.

With Christ's love. Jesus tells us, "My command is this: Love each other as I have loved you" (John 15:12). In our day and age we so readily psychologize the concept of love into "warm fuzzies" or sentimentalized slop. Jesus shows us that true love is action: treating each other the right way.

He adds, "Greater love has no one than this, that one lay down his life for his friends" (John 15:13). That's how he loved us. Not with flowery words or rosy intentions. He laid down his life for us. That's the kind of love he asks us to extend to each other.

According to God's commandments. The law of love alone does not guarantee that we will always treat each other the way we should. We cannot always determine for ourselves what the loving thing to do is in a given set of circumstances. For that reason God has given us his commandments to inform our actions. When we follow them not legalistically, but in the spirit of love, we have an unfailing guide to treating others right.

As I would treat Jesus himself. Jesus identifies so closely with his sheep that what we do to them, we do to him: "I tell you the truth, whatever you did for one of the least of these brothers of mine, you did for me" (Matt. 25:40). That shouldn't surprise us. Jesus is in heaven, but through his Spirit he accompanies his people every step of the way. When we dare to look into the eyes of his poor, we discover our opportunity to reach out and wipe away the tears of God.

With habitual forgiveness. When we pray "Forgive us our debts as we forgive our debtors," we're not pretending we should be weak-kneed, spineless wimps. We should boldly stand up to injustice, even that committed against ourselves.

But we must be quick to reconcile and forgive—not once, but as many times as it takes. Paul writes, " 'In your anger do not sin': Do not let the sun go down while you are still angry, and do not give the devil a foothold" (Eph. 4:26–27). Nothing so clearly shows the reality of God's grace in us as our ability to overcome our anger and hurt, forgiving each other from the heart.

The Church Says

By condemning envy, hatred, and anger
God tells us
   to love our neighbors as ourselves,
   to be patient, peace-loving, gentle,
      merciful, and friendly to them,
to protect them from harm as much as we can,
and to do good even to our enemies.

(Heidelberg Catechism A. 107)

Hotseat Question

Do you have unresolved hurts in your life? What should you do about them?

Check It Out

Matthew 5; 1 Corinthians 13; 1 John 3:11–24

QUEST
58

How do you determine what occupation God wants you to choose?

The average person can count on spending more than 80,000 hours on the job during his or her life. That's a lot of precious time, and it's important that we invest it wisely. But how can we be certain what kind of work God is calling us to do?

Some Possible Answers

I should consider my gifts. The Lord asks us to work with the talents he has given us. We should choose an occupation that will maximize their use. But before we can do that, we have to identify and develop our talents. That requires testing, trying out, and carefully evaluating the feedback we get from others. We need to discover our strengths as well as our weaknesses. In that way we gain important clues to where God wants us to spend our working lives.

I should look at the needs. Maybe the world already has enough art teachers, check-out clerks, or airline pilots. That's important to know before making career decisions. Because God's gifts should be used to supply the genuine needs in his world, we must find out where we can use our talents to best advantage for his kingdom.

I should look at my interests. Doing any job well requires us to develop some genuine interest. Every occupation gets tedious at times. After Adam's fall God's curse on work reminds us constantly that we still have a ways to go to reach the New Jerusalem. Nevertheless we can still find happiness in our work. Our genuine interest in our job helps us do it well.

I should look at the paycheck. It's important that we find work that allows us to provide for ourselves, for our dependents, and for God's poor, who cannot take care of their own needs. That's not a matter of optional charity, but of required justice. God promises, "If you spend yourselves in behalf of the hungry and satisfy the needs of the oppressed, then your light will rise in the darkness, and your night will become like the noonday. The Lord will guide you always; he will satisfy your needs" (Isa. 58:10–11).

I should determine how it fits in with my other responsibilities. God creates us to be more than just workers. He calls us to fulfill our responsibilities to family, friends, the community, and ourselves as well. If our work permanently crowds out these concerns, we need to look for other work because we've made our job into an idol.

The Church Says

**What does God require of you
in [the eighth] commandment?**

That I do whatever I can
for my neighbor's good,
that I treat others
as I would like them to treat me,
and that I work faithfully,
so that I may share with those in need.

(Heidelberg Catechism Q. & A. 111)

Hotseat Question

How does your chosen occupation fit in with your Christian witness?

Check It Out

Genesis 1:27–28; 2:15; Proverbs 6:6–11; Isaiah 58:5–12; Matthew 25:14–30

QUEST **59**	God requires you to live a chaste life. What does that mean to you?

The so-called sexual revolution has created some much-needed openness for discussing our sexuality. But is has also duped millions into believing that sexual sins are acceptable and even desirable. Whether you're single or married, God still asks you to live a morally pure life. Given your present marital status, what does God require of you?

Some Possible Answers

As a single person, it means that I reserve sexual intercourse for marriage. God made us sexual beings, and we need never shy away from that fact. However, the Bible clearly forbids us to engage in sexual intercourse outside of marriage. God intends this gift to enrich a fully mature, committed relationship, not a casual fling. Nor does he want us to use it to shore up a faltering romance.

Misusing our sexuality leads to pain outside of a relationship and confusion in an immature one. If we truly love someone, we do what's really right for that person: we build our relationship step by obedient step. God's way may be the hardest, but it's also the happiest.

It means that I don't wallow in indecency. Pornography hurts. Whether it comes in the form of glossy magazines or filthy talk, it injures us. It dirties our God-given sexuality and robs us of our dignity. The Bible shows us a better way. It tells us to stop idolizing sexual organs and to begin seeing each other as God intends: as sisters and brothers in Christ. Indecency poisons our relationships and cheapens our real bond in the Lord.

It means that "shacking up," trial marriages, open marriages, and homosexual activities are out. The Bible understands how strongly we may be tempted to form such relationships. That's why it warns us so sharply away from them. Such relationships just lead us further into the distortions that tear our lives apart. They exact an unacceptably high toll on us, on others, and on our God.

As a married person, it means that I remain faithful to my partner. Faithfulness in marriages requires more than avoiding sexual misconduct. It requires that husband and wife take time and effort to share and celebrate the intimacy God has given them. The opposite of faithfulness is not unfaithfulness but neglect.

It means that in every relationship I show appropriate love. Chastity means that we show that love, and only that love, which is appropriate to each of our relationships. We should love our parents in a very different way than we love our enemies. But in either case, we should be as Christ to them.

The Church Says

God condemns all unchastity.
   We should therefore thoroughly detest it
and, married or single,
live decent and chaste lives.
(Heidelberg Catechism A. 108)

We are temples of the Holy Spirit, body and soul,
and God wants both to be kept clean and holy.
That is why he forbids
   everything which incites unchastity,
   whether it be actions, looks, talk, thoughts, or desires.
(Heidelberg Catechism A. 109)

Hotseat Question

Can God forgive your sexual sins? Can you forgive yourself for these sins?

Check It Out

Romans 1:21–27; 1 Corinthians 6:12–20; 7:1–9

QUEST **60**	As a Christian, what kinds of talk are unworthy of you?

Sticks and stones may break my bones but words will never hurt me. Whoever invented that bit of nonsense did not read the Bible very carefully. James writes, "The tongue also is a fire, a world of evil among the parts of the body. It corrupts the whole person, sets the whole course of his life on fire, and is itself set on fire by hell" (James 3:6). We need buckets of God's purifying grace to clean out our mouths. As you monitor your speech, which sins do you find rolling easily off your tongue?

Some Possible Answers

Misusing God's Name. Dragging God's name through the mud provides an unacceptable, nasty way of responding to crisis situations. God strictly forbids it. Our heavenly Father asks us instead to stick up for his reputation in this world by telling others what he has done for us.

Lying. Deception comes naturally to us. We use it to manipulate, to cheat, and to duck our responsibilities. But Jesus asks us to discard this Satanic tool. Our Lord brought us from darkness into his light, where we no longer need to lie. His Spirit helps us to face the truth and to speak it in love.

Gossiping. What we say about others may fully correspond to fact and still be a lie. If what we whisper through the grapevine needlessly hurts others, we're guilty of being untruthful. Scripture tells us to hold our tongues instead of wagging them. If we can't say something upbuilding, we should be quiet.

Boasting. Whatever good we do, we do because God gave us the ability and the desire to do it. That eliminates any reason for us to boast. We know it. We confess it. But somehow, that BIG MOUTH of ours . . . !

Insulting. We're much too refined to physically beat people up. But with one deft stroke of our razor-sharp tongues we cut their self-respect to ribbons. A bloody nose or a black eye will heal. But the wounds our barbs inflict keep throbbing. Sticks and stones will only break bones. Words will destroy us.

Quarreling. Nothing wrong with a good, honest argument! Differences of opinion help us to sort out God's truth, the apostle Paul tells us. But when we allow differences to turn into divisions, we tear Christ's body apart.

We have to learn the right, the fitting words that lead to reconciliation. We can learn them from Jesus, who daily speaks such words on our behalf before his Father's throne.

The Church Says

[The third commandment] requires
    that we use the holy name of God
        only with reverence and awe,
    so that we may properly
        confess him,
        pray to him,
        and praise him in everything we do and say.
                            (*Heidelberg Catechism* A. *99*)

I should love the truth,
    speak it candidly,
    and openly acknowledge it.
And I should do what I can
    to guard and advance my neighbor's good name.
                            (*Heidelberg Catechism* A. *112*)

Hotseat Question

How many words do you speak per day? How many help others?

Check It Out

Exodus 20:7; Romans 1:28–32; Colossians 3:16–17; 1 Peter 3:8–16

Re-formed Roots

(Quests 61–65)

| QUEST **61** | Why do you want to make public profession of faith in a Reformed denomination? | *By saying yes to your Savior in a particular church, you are committing yourself to adult membership there. Out of all the many denominations and churches, you chose this one. Can you give some reasons for your choice?* |

Some Possible Answers

My parents raised me in this church. Unless we have definite reasons to make a break, it's probably a good idea to remain in the denomination in which we were raised. We don't pretend our church is the best, but we understand better how our church should grow in obedience to the Lord.

I like it here. While taste should not dictate which church we choose, it certainly plays a part. We can best serve and be served by a church in which we really feel at home.

Because this church has strong biblical preaching. Reformed preaching runs deep. Its power lies in its refusal to take shortcuts and cheap shots. It tries hard to explain the genuine intent of the Scriptures and apply it to our lives. Reformed preaching may not get high marks as entertainment, but it gives us solid spiritual food. It feeds us on Christ.

I agree with its teachings. The Reformed tradition shares the heart of the faith with all true churches. But we also have our own unique, doctrinal contribution to make to the rest of Christ's body. Our understanding of God's role in salvation, the meaning of sacraments, and the place of God's kingdom in this world sets us apart from other Christian traditions. Our interpretation of Scripture on such matters differs from theirs.

I like its strong covenantal emphasis. Reformed churches take God's covenant seriously. By baptizing infants, we recognize God's claim on our members from birth. We support parents in teaching their children the blessings and obligation of being God's kids. We provide a strong program of instruction to train young and old to serve our Lord better. And we supervise the spiritual development of our members through family visiting and Christian discipline.

I like its balance of Word and deed ministry. With the evangelicals, Reformed churches affirm the importance of evangelism. At the same time, we affirm with "mainline" churches the importance of helping the needy and poor in Christ's name. We do not see evangelism and diaconal work as opposites. We refuse to choose between being the hands or voice of Jesus: we want to be both.

The Church Says

This Synod of Dort in the name of the Lord pleads with all who devoutly call on the name of our Savior Jesus Christ to form their judgment about the faith of the Reformed churches, not on the basis of false accusations gathered from here or there, or even on the basis of the personal statements of a number of ancient and modern authorities . . . but on the basis of the churches' own official confessions.

(The Canons of Dort, Conclusion)

Hotseat Question

Which factor played the deciding role in your choice? Why?

Check It Out

1 Corinthians 1:18–25; 1 Corinthians 13; 2 John 4–11

QUEST **62**	**What truths held by the Protestant reformers mean the most to you?**

Through people such as Luther, Calvin, and Zwingli, the Lord corrected his badly blundering church. These reformers urged church leaders to submit to the clear teachings of Scripture. Church leaders responded by rejecting the ideas the reformers set forth and expelling these "protestants" from the Rome-ruled church. As Reformed Churches, we stand in the tradition of these reformers. We hold dear the truths they mined from God's Word. Which of these truths speak most strongly to you?

Some Possible Answers

I'm saved by grace alone. The Roman Church taught that Christ died only for our original sin. We somehow had to make up for our actual sins by doing good works, praying to saints, or having our souls purified in the fires of Purgatory.

Against the notion that we had to earn our own salvation to some degree, the reformers taught that Jesus paid the full price for all our sins. As Paul tells us, "For in the gospel a righteousness from God is revealed, a righteousness that is by faith from first to last, just as it is written: 'The righteous will live by faith' " (Rom. 1:17).

Scripture alone is my rule for faith and life. The Roman Church taught that Christians had to obey the pope and church tradition in addition to the Bible.

The reformers denied this. They accepted only God's Word as our infallible guide. Whatever teaching or leadership the church provides must always stand clearly under Scripture's norm, the reformers said. And the apostles need no successor on earth to exercise their authority. The Word they proclaimed is enough. Through it Christ rules his people until he returns.

Christ's sacrifice on Calvary is all-sufficient for me. The Roman Church taught that Christ's sacrifice on the cross was only the beginning; his body had to be resacrificed every day by the priests. As the priests blessed the bread and wine, claimed Roman church leaders, these elements turned into the actual body and blood of the Lord.

The Reformers denied this. They saw the elements shared by believers as symbols pointing back to Golgotha. By that remembrance, through the Spirit's power, believers find fellowship with their risen Lord.

The sovereignty of God. The Reformers rediscovered the biblical confession of God's active rule over all things. God, they maintained, does not just sit around waiting to see what we might do with the pieces of our broken lives. He takes the initiative, binding our rebellious hearts and lives back to him.

Far from relieving us of our responsibility, this doctrine calls us back to it. As Paul urges, "Continue to work out your salvation with fear and trembling, for it is God who works in you to will and to act according to his good purpose" (Phil. 2:12–13).

The Church Says

How are you right with God?

Only by true faith in Jesus Christ.

(Heidelberg Catechism Q. & A. 60)

God's judgment, both in this life and in the life to come,
   is based on [the] gospel testimony.

(Heidelberg Catechism A. 84)

The Lord's Supper declares to us
   that our sins have been completely forgiven
   through the one sacrifice of Jesus Christ
   which he himself finished on the cross once and for all.

(Heidelberg Catechism A. 80)

All creatures are so completely in [God's] hand
   that without his will
   they can neither move nor be moved.

(Heidelberg Catechism A. 28)

Hotseat Question

Was it worth splitting the church over these issues?

Check It Out

Job 42:1–6; Psalm 119:9–16; Philippians 3:7–11; Hebrews 10:10–18

QUEST **63**	Can you name and briefly summarize the three Reformation creeds?

Along with the Apostolic, Nicene, and Athanasian Creeds, most Reformed churches share three statements of faith that arose during the time of the Reformation. These we call doctrinal standards, because we use them to distinguish Reformed teaching from non-Reformed teaching. Your church may call you, as a confessing member, to office and ask you to sign your agreement with these doctrinal standards. Can you name them and summarize their content?

Some Possible Answers

The Belgic Confession. A preacher named Guido de Brès wrote this confession in 1561 in Belgium, then still part of the Southern Netherlands. The Roman Catholic government had launched a smear campaign against the Reformed Church, accusing them of treason and heresy. In his confession de Brès clearly refutes these charges and states what Reformed Christians believe.

De Brès's efforts failed to stop the persecution, and he himself was hanged. But the Reformed churches adopted a revised version of his beautiful testimony as their own.

We can outline this confession as follows:

Articles   1–11: God and His Revelation
12–15: Creation and Fall
16–26: Christ and Salvation
27–35: Church and Government
36: Civil Government
37: Last Judgment

The Heidelberg Catechism. Zacharius Ursinus, a theology professor, and Caspar Olevianus, a court preacher, completed this catechism in 1563 at the request of Frederick III. Frederick was prince of the Palatinate province, of which Heidelberg was the capital.

The word *catechism* means "echo." Because few people could read or write in those days, the best way to teach was to have students echo back short answers, committing them to memory. The Heidelberg Catechism was written to help pastors teach the basics of the faith to youth. Later it was divided into fifty-two "Lord's Days" for use in Sunday worship as well.

The Heidelberg Catechism divides into three main parts:

Introductory Summary:	Lord's Day 1
Part 1: Man's Misery:	Lord's Days 2-4
Part 2: Man's Deliverance:	Lord's Days 5-31
Part 3: Man's Gratitude:	Lord's Days 32-52

Within this structure the catechism weaves four things new communicants were expected to know: the Apostolic Creed, the sacraments, the Ten Commandments, and The Lord's Prayer.

The Canons of Dort. The word *canon* in this context means a "rule of doctrine laid down by the church." In 1618–19 delegates from the Reformed churches met in the city of Dordrecht, the Netherlands, to settle a dispute over the teachings of a theologian named Jacob Arminius. These canons make up the official response of the synod in which it refutes his teachings.

The canons affirm five points of doctrine:

T - Total Depravity (pt. III/IV)—sin has affected every part of our nature.

U - Unconditional Election (pt. I)—God chose us in Christ, apart from our own merits or foreseen faith.

L - Limited Atonement (pt. II)—Christ's death is sufficient for all, efficient only for the elect.

I - Irresistible Grace (pt. III/IV)—We come to saving faith only because God breaks through our rejection of him.

P - Perseverance of the Saints: (pt. V)—God preserves his own, assuring them that they will always be his.

Hotseat Question

What should you do if you disagree with what these confessions teach?

Check It Out

Romans 10:5–13; 1 John 4:1–6

<table>
<tr><td>

QUEST

64

</td><td>

How does
Reformed
church
government
differ from
other
church
structures?

</td><td>

*Today we witness a bewildering number
of denominations and independent
congregations. Despite their many
differences, all these churches tend to
structure themselves in one of three
ways. What are these forms of
government and which of them do
Reformed churches follow?*

</td></tr>
</table>

Some Possible Answers

Some function from the top down. The Roman Catholic, Anglican, and
Orthodox churches have adopted a hierarchical structure of church
government. Christ, they believe, delegates full authority over all the
churches to his representative on earth. Below this person are the
archbishops, bishops, priests, and rank-and-file members, in descending
order of importance.

  Higher-ups appoint the leaders that serve under their jurisdiction. The
average pew-warmer has no vote and little say in this process. Local
churches are extensions of the denomination itself and are fully under its
control in all matters.

  Today many priests do appoint boards and committees to oversee specific
tasks in the parish, but these groups have no authority of their own.

Some function from the bottom up. Most evangelical churches, such as
Baptists, Methodists, and Pentecostals, use a democratic structure in which
final authority rests with the members of the individual congregations.
Members choose their own leaders and decide major issues by common
consent. These churches may form loose relationships within a
denominational structure, but individual congregations retain full autonomy.

Reformed churches adopt a middle position: rule by elder. Paul advises Titus,
"Appoint elders in every town, as I directed you" (Titus 1:5). From texts such
as this Reformed and Presbyterian churches adopt what they consider to be
the biblical model: rule by officers. Together officebearers, chosen from
among the members, form the church council. Through this group Christ
rules his people. Although the council may invite the advice of members on
important issues, council alone has final say in congregational matters.

Though each church regulates its own internal affairs through its council, Reformed churches establish close ties with the other congregations in their denomination. Councils regularly delegate representatives to classis and synod. These wider bodies are given authority to make decisions on issues of shared interest. In this way all congregations are presumed equal. None may lord it over the other. Yet these congregations cooperate closely by accepting the leadership of the wider assemblies on matter of common concern.

The Church Says

We believe that
ministers of the Word of God, elders, and deacons
ought to be chosen to their offices
by a legitimate election of the church,
with prayer in the name of the Lord,
and in good order,
   as the Word of God teaches.

As for the ministers of the Word,
they all have the same power and authority,
   no matter where they may be,
since they are all servants of Jesus Christ,
   the only universal bishop,
   and the only head of the church.

(Belgic Confession Article 31)

Hotseat Question

What can you do to support the leadership in your church?

Check It Out

Matthew 18:15–20; Mark 10:42–45; Acts 20:25–28

QUEST 65

As Reformed people we emphasize the lordship of Christ over all of life. What does that mean to you?

Every Christian operates with a worldview—a way of understanding what life is all about. Many mentally carve the world up into two parts: the spiritual and the physical. They consider the spiritual all-important. That's the area of life concerning our relationship to God, our souls, and the afterlife. Our everyday existence has little lasting value. In contrast, the Reformed faith teaches that life is of one piece. God created all of it. He cares about all of it. Jesus saves all of it. And he rules not only our souls but also our bodies. What might this Reformed view mean for the way you look at the world?

Some Possible Answers

That all of my life is sacred. Nothing in our lives is religiously neutral. Jesus is Lord of our tennis playing as well as our Bible reading. In every area of life he calls us to respond obediently to his command to love God above all and our neighbor as ourselves. This means that our daily work is and should be kingdom work. Not only preachers receive their calling from God. We all do: farmers, homemakers, plumbers, and artists. The other things we do in life—visit, play, eat, and study—we also dedicate to his service.

The real conflict in my life is between my old self and new self, not between body and soul. The real struggle in our lives is not between a polluted body and a perfect soul trapped inside it. Sin poisoned both. Yet together soul and body belong to Christ, and he will restore both of them.

The real battle rages between our old nature and our new nature. Our old, sinful self keeps trying to regain control of our life. But Jesus helps us nail it to the cross of self-denial. There it cannot harm us if we follow him—body and soul.

We need to extend Christ's claim into every area of life. We may not bottle the kingdom of heaven up behind solid oak church doors. Jesus asks us to represent him everywhere: in the marketplace, the theater, and the office. Our king calls us to action in every area of life—in politics, labor, technology, and the arts. All areas offer opportunities for communal Christian action and witness.

We recognize the crucial importance of Christian education to equip us for this life-embracing task. Parental instruction, church education, Christian schools and universities, are all ways in which we can equip God's ambassadors to live out their conviction that our whole world belongs to God.

The Church Says

Your kingdom come means,

Rule us by your Word and Spirit in such a way
    that more and more we submit to you.

Keep your church strong, and add to it.

Destroy the devil's work;
destroy every force which revolts against you
and every conspiracy against your Word.

Do this until your kingdom is so complete and perfect
    that in it you are
        all in all.

                                              (Heidelberg Catechism A. 123)

Hotseat Question

Where can you involve yourself in fruitful Christian action?

Check It Out

Romans 8:18–25; Ephesians 1:19–23; Colossians 1:15–23